Martin Luther King Jr.

4

Schulke, Flip

King remembered

DATE DUE

Underlining 2 WEEKS
noted 10/7/96

KING
REMEMBERED

Flip Schulke
Penelope Ortner McPhee

W. W. Norton & Company
New York • London

Book Design by Robert S. Nemser

Photograph credit and copyright holders:

1986 © Flip Schulke: pages ii and iii, xiv, 3, 12, 17 (both), 19, 22, 26–27, 30, 32, 37, 42, 47, 49, 52, 61 (both), 62, 64, 68, 69 (both), 70 (both), 73 (both), 81, 87, 92, 97, 108, 112, 121, 124 (both), 130 (both), 135, 136, 137, 140, 146–47, 148–49, 151, 152, 153, 156, 160, 165, 166 (both), 167, 168, 172 (both), 173, 173 (right), 174 (left), 180, 184, 186, 191, 192, 195, 198–99, 200–201, 201 (right), 202–3, 204, 205, 208, 209, 210, 211, 212, 216, 220, 221, 222–23, 224, 225, 228, 229, 231, 232, 237, 243, 248, 252, 255, 257, 260, 261, 263, 264, 268, 269, 271, 272, 275.

1986 © Declan Haun: pages vii, 8, 159, 256.

1986 © Ivan Massar: pages 113, 206.

1986 © Dan McCoy–Black Star: page 7 (top).

1986 © Charles Moore–Black Star: pages 7 (bottom), 128–29, 130 (bottom), 131, 185, 188–89.

1986 © Robert Fitch–Black Star, page 76.

1986 © Lee Lockwood–Black Star, page 102.

Copyright © Time-Inc., Joseph Louw, Time Picture agency, page 247.

Photographs courtesy of: Wide World, 39; U.S. Department of the Interior, 145; Lyndon Baines Johnson Library—Cecil Stoughton, 178; Yoichi Okamoto, 207; Schulke Archives, 6, 28, 56, 57, 84–85, 86, 91, 98, 104, 105, 109, 116—Rev. Wyatt Tee Walker; 174–175, 236, 238, 242, 276—Rev. Wyatt Tee Walker.

Text Copyright © 1986, Penelope O. McPhee

The following material is reprinted by permission of Harper & Row Publishers, Inc.: "Letter from Birmingham Jail," April 16, 1983, in *Why Can't We Wait* by Martin Luther King, Jr., © 1963 by Martin Luther King, Jr.

Excerpts from the following speeches and sermons are used by permission of Joan Daves: "I've Been to the Mountaintop," © 1968 by Estate of Martin Luther King, Jr.; "Nobel Prize Acceptance," © 1964 by The Nobel Foundation; "Riverside Church-Vietnam," © 1968 by Estate of Martin Luther King, Jr.; "Drum Major Instinct," © 1968 by Estate of Martin Luther King, Jr.; "Harlem Armory Speech," © 1964 by Martin Luther King, Jr.; "Detroit Freedom March," © 1963 by Martin Luther King, Jr.

Published simultaneously in Canada by Penguin Books Canada Ltd, 2801 John Street, Markham, Ontario L3R 1B4
Printed in the United States of America.

The text of this book is composed in 13 point Souvenir Light, with display type set in 40 point Souvenir Demi-bold. Composition and manufacturing by The Maple-Vail Book Manufacturing Group.

Library of Congress Cataloging-in-Publication Data

Schulke, Flip.
  King remembered.

  Includes index.
  1. King, Martin Luther. 2. Afro-Americans—Biography. 3. Baptists—United States—Clergy—Biography. 4. Afro-Americans—Civil rights.
I. McPhee, Penelope Ortner. II. Title.
E185.97.K5S38   1986   323.4′092′4 [B] 85–22172

ISBN 0-393-02256-0

W. W. Norton & Company, Inc., 500 Fifth Avenue, New York, N.Y. 10110

W. W. Norton & Company Ltd., 37 Great Russell Street, London WC1B 3NU

2 3 4 5 6 7 8 9 0

CONTENTS

Dedication

To the devoted colleagues of Dr. Martin Luther King, Jr., who continue the nonviolent struggle to achieve his dream of the Beloved Community, and who so generously shared with the authors their memories of the past, their goals for the future, and the spirit of the movement.

Foreword

by Jesse Jackson

It is a special joy for me to introduce a book about my friend and mentor, Dr. Martin Luther King, Jr. I am keenly aware that were it not for the vision and courage of Dr. King, I might not be writing these words at all, much less as someone who ran for the highest office in the land. Even today, nearly two decades after his death, doors that once were closed and locked are still being opened because of the legacy of Dr. King.

Yet mixed with the joy and enthusiasm of writing about Dr. King is a sense of humility as I realize that no words I write could adequately capture the contribution that he made to world peace in his all-too-brief life. There is a saying in Spanish that roughly translates into, "Tell me who you are associated with, and I will tell you who you are." In the case of Dr. King, perhaps it is enough to say that his name is often mentioned in the same breath as Jesus Christ and Mohandas Gandhi. Those associations say most of what needs to be said about Martin Luther King, Jr.

These days I often lecture on college campuses. I am constantly struck by the opportunities that those fortunate enough to attend college will have upon graduation. Many will be able to afford fine cars and clothes. But will they choose personal wealth or the public's health? Will they choose a luxurious car, or will they give a ride to the stranger who has lost his way? Will they choose the latest in European fashions, or will they choose to clothe the naked? The Bible teaches us that we judge character by how we treat the least of these; that we judge a tree not by the bark but by the fruit it bears.

Our society has elevated greed and profit to sanctified levels. In 1984 ninety thousand corporations made a profit and paid no taxes; one hundred thousand individuals made one hundred thousand dollars or more and paid no taxes, while folks making two thousand dollars below the poverty level paid taxes.

Books make the best-seller list and classes are filled to capacity that aim to teach us hundreds of ways to avoid paying taxes. But no one can teach us how to love and to share, to care for the less fortunate. If we study the life and example of Dr. King, however, like those of Gandhi and Jesus, we learn that these values of love and generosity and unselfishness were what motivated them. They were great not because they were well known—Hitler is well known. They were great because they served the cause of peace and justice for all of the human family. Indeed, their commitment to better the human condition led them to give their very lives in such service.

The same misguided values that motivate many to seek personal wealth have also led our nation to squander precious resources. Perhaps no area of national policy better illustrates this point than our rising military budget. Our trillion dollar deficit is in no small measure related to the unbridled escalation in defense spending. What's more, we spend more on military hardware every day and yet we are less secure than ever in our history. Defense spending generates fewer jobs than other areas of spending. It produces nothing of utility to our society—no food, no clothes, no housing, no medical supplies or equipment, in short, nothing of social value. Yet each year we spend more on the military budget and cut spending on health, housing, and education to make up the difference.

These are the battles that Martin would be waging were he alive today. That is why he was one of the first to openly oppose United States' involvement in Viet Nam. He was on the right side of history. Today he would demand that we cut defense spending without cutting our defenses. It can be done. During the presidential campaign, I outlined a program that would cut defense spending by 20 percent and would have left us no less secure than we are today. Dr. King's memory deserves a safer and a saner world.

Martin celebrated his last birthday on this earth working to achieve his vision of a caring and just society. I was with him on that day in the Ebenezer Baptist Church in Atlanta, which he spent organizing the Poor People's March on Washington.

Shortly before he died, Martin reminded us what is important and what is not. "When I die," he said, "don't build a monument to me. Don't bestow on me degrees from great universities. Just say I tried to clothe the naked. Say that I tried to house the homeless. Let people say that I tried to feed the hungry." And he did. We all did. America responded to the challenge. We expanded the school lunch program for children and food stamps for poor families. We started a supplemental feeding program called Women, Infants and Children (WIC) for pregnant mothers and their babies, and we created meals programs for our elderly citizens.

Ten years later doctors went into the same states where hunger and malnutrition had been rampant a decade before. Hunger was virtually eliminated. But it is no longer the sixties or the seventies. It is the eighties, and hunger and malnutrition have returned as serious problems in America. Parents with babies, young children, and the elderly line up at soup kitchens throughout this nation because they are hungry. Think of it if you will: the embarrassing and ugly spectre of breadlines running across the wealthiest nation on earth! Today we have a crisis in America. We are a nation adrift. Our spiritual power and the power of our people is in jeopardy. And nothing better exemplifies this crisis than the presence of hunger in a nation of plenty.

Martin would remind us that now is the time for leadership. It is now that we decide whether the B-1 Bomber is more important than a child's school lunch program. Now is the time to decide whether the MX missile gives us more security than the nutrition programs which feed our families and the elderly. If we eliminate two CVN Nuclear Attack Carriers, which cost $3.4 billion each, we can take that $7 billion and restore every federal nutrition program cut by the Reagan Administration. We will have enough money left over to increase food stamp benefits by 25 percent and still have enough money left to expand the school lunch program. That would be a tribute worthy of Dr. King.

We do not have a resource problem. We have a priority problem that is ultimately a moral problem. We have enough resources, but we squander them on bogus security and military madness. Our security, in the final analysis, is in our people and their well-being.

That most secure line of defense from foreign invasion and ideology, as Dr. King would have reminded us, is a people who are well-fed and well-read.

That is really what Dr. Martin Luther King, Jr., sought to tell this nation and our leaders. He recognized that we are a compassionate nation and a decent people. But sometimes our leaders do not reflect our decency and compassion in their public policies, and when they fail it is incumbent upon us to lead them back to those policies which reflect our most fundamental beliefs. This is a time when our leadership has strayed far from the best of our nation's tradition and instead has led us back to those times when racial and economic discrimination were codified in the very law of the land. Martin is no longer with us. But his example is. We must learn from it and follow it. For when it is dark outside the stars shine brightest. Let Martin be the star that shines for our nation.

A final note. In the two decades since his death, I have seen Dr. King's image all too often reshaped to conform to what some would prefer for us to remember about him. Depictions of him as a pacifist and a humanist often are tinged with the implication that he eschewed confrontation and aggressiveness. But those of us who knew him and worked with him were never confused about his goals or his tactics and strategies. Of course Dr. King promoted peace and harmony among all of God's children. Of course he preferred negotiation over confrontation and friendly persuasion over state decree. But Martin understood that change seldom comes that way. He realized that the powerful seldom relinquish privilege without a struggle. Hence, his was an active and aggressive civil disobedience. He deplored violence not only because it was un-Christian but also because he knew it was a prescription for genocide. Martin was an idealist who had his feet planted firmly in reality. Martin knew that if change was to come, he would have to suffer. But he was not afraid, because he knew that suffering breeds character, and character breeds faith. And in the end, faith will not disappoint.

Read and learn about Dr. Martin Luther King, Jr. But do not stop there, for he would not have. Apply the lessons of his life and his example as we rededicate ourselves to fulfilling his dream. There is much work yet to be done.

October 1985
Chicago, Illinois

Authors' Preface

Martin Luther King, Jr., joins Christopher Columbus, George Washington, and Abraham Lincoln to become only the fourth man in our nation's history to have a national holiday established in his honor. This book is written in the belief that if the holiday that commemorates Martin Luther King's place in history is to be meaningful—more than an empty tribute—it must provide us with an opportunity to study both an exceptional man who is no longer with us and a philosophy that remains very much alive.

Since the publication of our first book, *Martin Luther King, Jr.: A Documentary . . . Montgomery to Memphis,* each of us has had many opportunities to speak about King and the civil rights movement to students from elementary school to college level. We are often dismayed to find that many younger people—both black and white—do not understand the importance of King's contribution. They know that, somehow, he was a "great man." They do not know why! It is both a tribute and a tragedy that many of King's achievements are already taken for granted. In many places in the South, an entire generation has no concept of the extent of the segregation King encountered and eradicated.

The principal basis for this book is the collective memory of those who knew Dr. King, who worked beside him, who influenced him, and who were, in their turn, influenced by him. Not for one moment have these committed men and women wavered from the cause of human rights or the method of nonviolence. Today each of them continues to contribute in his own special way, but they are unified by a spiritual bond that was forged in their years of marching with Martin Luther King. They remain an inspiration to all of us to continue to work for King's dream of a Beloved Community and to communicate his teachings to others.

Their recollections of Dr. King as he actually was are an irreplaceable repository of King's legacy. As such, they are infinitely precious and frighteningly perishable. We believe that they should be recorded and communicated while they are still available to us. Should we miss this opportunity to capture the reality of Martin Luther King as he was known and remembered by his closest associates, a vital part of our national consciousness and our national conscience might be irrevocably lost to us, to our children, and to succeeding generations.

Each of us—one a photojournalist, the other an author and television producer—has come to this mission by separate and strikingly divergent paths.

Flip Schulke knew Martin Luther King personally and intimately. He first met Dr. King in the late 1950s on assignment for *Jet* magazine. At that first meeting, King and Schulke talked about the importance of photographing events as they happened. Schulke convinced King that it was essential to document every aspect of the civil rights movement, and subsequently, Schulke became one of the few photographers to cover the entire southern civil rights struggle. Ultimately, King gained a trust in Schulke that was never betrayed.

By contrast, Penelope McPhee never met Dr. King in person. In fact, she was still a college student when Martin Luther King was assassinated. "Black Power" had become a strong focus of the black movement, and many well-meaning whites did not know exactly where they fit in the civil rights picture. For McPhee, the answer came as she immersed herself in the teachings and philosophy of Martin Luther King, while researching and writing our first book, *Montgomery to Memphis.*

For both of us, King offered a solution to the injustices we saw around us. King believed in the goodness of man; he believed in human dignity, in individuality, in community. His concern was not only for the rights of blacks, but also for women, for the poor, for all the disadvantaged. And he demonstrated to us that we all have a positive power to change our circumstances.

Martin Luther King's dream is not yet a reality. With all of its potential, America still has not achieved "liberty and justice for all." But King believed we as a people could change. He left us a vision of what we and our society might be and a means of achieving that vision. He showed us the best we can be.

King insisted that man is esentially good and that we behave badly only when our experiences and circumstances teach us to violate the proper ethical conduct that is innate in each of us. Central to all of King's actions, writings, speeches, and sermons was the concept that by making men aware of the evil of their ways, they would change their behavior. And, therefore, it is up to all of us to continue to try to teach and to communicate. That is the challenge Dr. King left for us and the inspiration for this book.

Flip Schulke
Penelope O. McPhee

Acknowledgments

The authors wish to express their appreciation to the many individuals who contributed their time and creativity to this project. We are extremely grateful to Starling Lawrence, our editor at W. W. Norton and Company, for his suggestions, his patience, and his confidence. We would also like to thank his associates Jill Bialosky and Hilary Hinzmann.

We particularly want to thank Coretta Scott King for creating the Martin Luther King, Jr., Center for Nonviolent Social Change and making its library and archives available to authors such as ourselves.

Our deepest thanks to Reverend C. T. Vivian, not only for sharing his memories with us, but also for his assistance in arranging many of our other personal interviews, and to his wife, Octavia, whose historical files and records were extremely helpful. We would also like to thank Reverend Ralph Abernathy, Congressman Walter Fauntroy, Reverend Jesse Jackson, Mayor Andrew Young, Senator Julian Bond, Dr. Joseph Lowery, Reverend Fred Shuttlesworth, Councilman John Lewis, Burke Marshall, Reverend Hosea Williams, and Jo Ann Robinson for granting us lengthy personal interviews.

Our appreciation to Robert Nemser for his art direction, and to Howard Chapnick, Black Star Picture Agency, for encouraging photography of the civil rights struggle and for his decisive picture editing of this book. Thanks are also due Herbert Nipson, editor, and John H. Johnson, publisher, of *Jet* and *Ebony,* who gave Flip Schulke his first assignments on Dr. King.

Our thanks to Louise Cook, director of the library and archives of the Martin Luther King, Jr., Center for Nonviolent Social Change in Atlanta, Georgia, for her research assistance; to Black Star photographers whose works appear as credited: Charles Moore, Robert Fitch, Dan McCoy, Lee Lockwood, and Ivan Massar; to White House photographers Cecil Stoughton and the late Yoichi Okamoto. We are especially grateful to photojournalist Declan Haun. Most of the photographs in this book were printed by Modernage Labs, New York. We extend our appreciation to Wolfram Kloetz for the extra effort and care taken in printing. For her careful transcription of more than thirty hours of personal interviews, our thanks to Kristie Abart. We would like, too, to acknowledge the research assistance we received from the Lyndon Baines Johnson Library in Austin, Texas.

Finally, our heartfelt thanks to both of our spouses, who contributed their professional expertise as well as their loving encouragement. To Debra Streuber Schulke for her help in picture research and picture editing and to Raymond Hunter McPhee for his thoughtful reading of the manuscript and his wise editorial suggestions.

KING
REMEMBERED

MARTIN LUTHER KING, JR.
WAS BORN IN THIS HOUSE
JANUARY 15, 1929

Chapter One

The
Heritage

*We see men as Jews or Gentiles, Catholics
or Protestants, Chinese or Americans, Negroes
or whites. We fail to think of them as fellow
human beings made from the same basic stuff
as we, molded in the same divine image.*

MLK, Jr.

MARTIN LUTHER KING, JR., came silently into the world on the morning of January 15, 1929. Alberta King's pregnancy and labor had been difficult, and for a moment the child lay so quietly those in attendance thought him stillborn. Perhaps he was reluctant to accept the heritage to which he was being born—that of a black child in white America.

Through an error, the first son of Alberta and Martin Luther King, Sr., was listed officially as Michael Luther King, Jr., and that remained his name of record until he applied for his first passport in 1957. From the beginning, he was Martin to his father, as later he would be to the world. But he was M. L. or Mike to childhood friends and family.

He grew up in a two-story Victorian frame house on Atlanta's Auburn Avenue. The Kings and their neighbors were successful middle-class professionals and businessmen. They had little in common with the poor blacks in Atlanta's ghetto, but they shared a bond that made them brothers—the darkness of their skin. Although Atlanta was a segregated southern city, it had a history of tolerance toward its black population. The Kings' street, known affectionately as "Sweet Auburn," sloped from the famous Peachtree Street into a valley that contained some of the largest Negro-owned businesses in America—insurance companies, newspapers, and banks among them.

Martin, Jr.,'s father, "Daddy King" to his family, was a highly respected member of this thriving community. The elder King had been born in poverty on a plantation outside Atlanta, one of ten children. He was still a boy when he left the cotton fields where his father was a sharecropper. Carrying his one pair of shoes, he walked barefoot to Atlanta, where he doggedly worked his own way through high school and ultimately entered Morehouse College. While still a student, he began preaching at two small churches in Atlanta. It was during this time that he met and married Alberta, the attractive daughter of Adam Daniel Williams, one of the leading black pastors of the city. Reverend A. D. Williams had built Ebenezer Baptist Church into a major institution and was its pastor for thirty-seven years. When he died, his son-in-law became pastor of what was already becoming the family church.

King, Sr., also took up his father-in-law's mantle as a leader of those blacks in Atlanta who opposed the indignities of segregation. Reverend Williams had led a successful boycott of an Atlanta newspaper when it called a black citizens' group "dirty and ignorant."

Martin Luther King, Jr.,'s parents,
Reverend Martin Luther King, Sr., and
Alberta Williams King.

The tactic helped force the newspaper into bankruptcy. His son-in-law, Reverend King, Sr., continued to set an example of resistance to segregation that was not lost on his eldest son. Martin's father became a power in the local NAACP and the Atlanta Negro Voters League. He refused to ride segregated buses, fought for equal pay for black teachers, and forced desegregation of elevators in Atlanta's courthouse. "Even though the law may force me to ride in the back, my mind is always up front," he would say to his son.

In the words of Arthur Henderson, who was married by Reverend King, Sr., and has long served as a deacon of Ebenezer Baptist Church, Martin King "had a beautiful beginning because of his background—his grandfather and his father. Really, the groundwork had been laid."

Daddy King was a proud man and would prove to be a strong influence on Martin, Jr. The young son very early shared the father's sense of outrage at injustice and pride in himself and his race. Later in life he would recall several incidents from his childhood that helped define his attitudes about himself and about being black. He remembered once, as a small boy, being taken by his father to a white establishment to buy shoes. They sat on a bench in the front of the store. When a clerk asked the father and son to move to the rear to be waited on, Reverend King refused, saying they would either buy shoes sitting where they were or not at all. Then, taking his son by the hand, he marched out the door. On another occasion, Martin was in the car with his father when a policeman stopped them, claiming Reverend King had run a stop sign. "All right, boy . . . ," the officer began. The pastor interrupted indignantly, "I'm no boy," and pointing to his small son said, *"This* is a boy. I am a man."

Martin learned dignity from his father, who never forgot the humiliation and subservience of life on the plantation and never resigned himself to it. If he taught his son a single lesson, it was "you are as good as anybody else." And it was Martin's nature to believe him.

"After I decided to enter the ministry, he constantly stressed the need for leadership," King was later to say of his father, "and I'm sure that he hoped I would stand out in this area. Whether he realized that I would do it or not is something else, but he certainly hoped for this."

"He was always a very sensitive child," his father recalled, "and always above his age in his thinking and in his carriage. I wouldn't say he was a peculiar child, but he was a little different in that he always made friends with good books from a small child."

Recognizing his early aptitude, his mother enrolled Martin in first grade before the mandatory age of six. But even though he could already read, he was expelled when teachers and administrators learned his true age. "He came home very much upset," recollected his father, "saying that the teacher told him he wasn't old enough; he'd have to wait another year at least before he could go to school."

"I told you so, I told you they wouldn't let you go to school," taunted his sister Christine. "You better hush your mouth, or I'll beat you up," Martin said angrily. He already felt a fierce academic competition with his year-older sibling.

"He was determined that his sister wouldn't finish school before he did," remembered his father, "so he skipped. He never did take the twelfth grade. He skipped from eleventh, took the examination and went on to college. They entered college together, and they both finished in 1948, the same year. So he kept his word."

From his schoolteacher mother, Martin inherited a patience and deliberateness that would later enable him to wait out his adversaries and turn the other cheek. From both parents, the King children learned the importance of courtesy, discipline, honesty, and hard work. "Coming up in a minister's home," he later recalled, "I faced the discipline that you would face in a fervent religious background."

Life revolved around family, church, and job. At eight, M. L. had a newspaper route, and by the time he was thirteen, he was the youngest assistant manager of a delivery station for the *Atlanta Journal*. But no matter how hard he worked, he could progress no further. Only white men could advance to the position of station manager.

Martin, Christine, and their younger brother, Alfred Daniel (named partly after his maternal grandfather), were in grade school before they felt the bitter sting of discrimination firsthand. Like all black children in the South, they knew there were places forbidden to them—certain water fountains and rest rooms they could not use; certain restaurants and stores where they were not welcome; certain seats on a bus or in a movie theatre where they could not sit; swimming pools, parks, and playgrounds where they could not join the games. But theirs was a privileged childhood in many ways. Circumstances had protected them from the worst of Jim Crow's indignities. So it was a shock to Martin, when he reached school

WHITE ONLY
←LADIES→
REST ROOM

*Blacks in the South faced
the overt hostility of white
racists and the indignities
of Jim Crow laws.*

REALM NATIONAL ALABAMA

KKKK

U.S. KLAN K.K.K.K. INC.

CAPITOL CITY
KLAVERNS
#104-23-125
WELCOME YOU

To King, it was apparent that southern blacks had been deprived of "human rights and plunged into searing poverty generation after generation."

age, that he was forbidden to play with two of his closest childhood friends, who happened to be white.

"None of us," King recalled, "seriously thought anything about those white boys being different, and we played with them all the time until we were ready for school. Well, they went to the white school and I went to another, and I still didn't think much about it at first. But suddenly when I would run across the street after school to compare notes, their mother would tell them that they could not play anymore. She said they were white and I was colored. At first, she just made excuses, but finally she told me. I think I cried, but anyway I rushed home and asked my mother about it."

And so his education in bigotry and hate, discrimination and injustice began. His mother and grandmother tried to explain to him in the gentlest way possible about slavery and segregation and being black in America. "Don't let this thing make you feel you're not as good as white people," his mother concluded. "You're as good as anyone else, and don't you forget it."

But even the most loving assurances of a mother and grandmother could not protect an unsuspecting child from the surprise attacks of white prejudice. Once, while Martin stood in front of an Atlanta store waiting for his mother, a total stranger slapped him across the face. "That little nigger stepped on my foot," the woman said.

Endeavoring to understand this kind of cruelty and humiliation, M. L. began to read avidly about the history of his people, about slavery and the Civil War, about such black men as Frederick Douglass, Nat Turner, Denmark Vesey, and Booker T. Washington. "He read everything he could on these things," said his father. "He was making preparations. He was organized within himself."

"On the one hand, my mother taught me that I should feel a sense of somebodiness," Martin explained. "On the other hand, I had to go out and face the system, which stared me in the face everyday, saying, 'You are less than.' 'You are not equal to.' So this was a real tension within."

He was still in elementary school when he came home from an outing with his father and told his mother, "Daddy got in an argument with a white man, and he told the white man he didn't have nerve enough to pull the trigger." Knowing that this upset his mother, he added, "You know, when I get to be a man, I'm going to hit this thing, and hit it hard, Mother; there's no such thing as one people better than another. The Lord made us all equal, and I'm going to see to that."

Reverend T. J. Jimerson, a lifelong friend of the King family, understood the root of King's drive and motivation. "The Christian rearing had given him a burning desire that the whites could not understand. It was sort of like a peace that the world can't give and the world can't take away. Because of his early rearing, he had been always taught to have faith in God and be afraid of no man. This was his father's point of view and he had transferred it over to his sons. And, of course, for him to have led and to have gotten into the thick of the thing is no surprise to anyone who knew Martin Luther King, Jr., from the very beginning of his life. He had always been like that, even as a student. He was quiet, and whenever he spoke, he spoke with assurance and with authority."

From an early age, he cultivated the words that would be his tool. No doubt two generations of fundamentalist ministry gave Martin a special sense of language—the cadence and rhythm of words that were to become his trademark. Upon hearing the sermon of a particularly eloquent minister as a youngster, he told his parents, "Someday I'm going to have me some big words like that." He always held his own in an argument, but although he preferred to fight verbally, he was not a boy to shy away from a physical confrontation. On occasion with his playmates, he would "go to the grass" to wrestle out a dispute. His childhood friends remember him as strong, stockily built, and excelling at football and other games despite his small stature.

His family remembers him stoically taking whatever punishment was meted out to him in childhood. Although it was a family custom for the children to spank one another for misbehavior, Martin tried to avoid having to punish his brother and flatly refused to hit his sister. Frequently, too, he refused to defend himself in boyhood quarrels, being inclined instead to turn the other cheek and accept the blows. "I hadn't thought of nonviolence at that early age, as a system of thought or a practical technique," he himself admitted. "I think a great part of it was that I just wouldn't dare retaliate or hit back when a white person was involved, and I think some of it was a part of my native structure so to speak, that I have never been one to hit back too much."

Even as a teenager, he was consciously developing the oratorical skills with which he would arm himself. His interest in debate and public speaking grew in high school, and when he was fourteen, he won an oratorical contest sponsored by the Negro Elks. His subject was the Negro and the constitution. Returning from the contest in Dublin, Georgia, Martin and his teacher, Mrs. Bradley, sat in the first available seats on the bus. "At a small town along the way, some white passengers boarded the bus, and the white driver ordered us to get up and give the whites our seats. We didn't move quickly enough to suit him, so he began cursing us, calling us 'black sons of bitches.' I intended to stay right in that seat," recalled Martin, "but Mrs. Bradley finally urged me up, saying we had to obey the law. And so we stood up in the aisle for the ninety miles to Atlanta. That night will never leave my memory. It was the angriest I have ever been in my life."

In many ways, Martin was a typical teenager. He liked chasing girls, adored dancing, and was so vain about his clothes he was given the nickname "Tweed." But as a student he was far above average and old beyond his years. He was accepted at Morehouse College, his father's alma mater and one of the best black colleges in the country, when he was only fifteen.

As he prepared to enter college, he seemed to his mother remarkably mature. He had an unusual seriousness and resolve, and he was determined to become a lawyer. "I was at that point," he explained later, "where I was deeply interested in political matters and social ills. I could envision myself playing a part in breaking down the legal barriers to Negro rights."

Chapter Two

The
Path

I came to see for the first time that the Christian doctrine of love, operating through the Gandhian method of nonviolence, is one of the most potent weapons available to an oppressed people in their struggle for freedom.

MLK, Jr.

MOREHOUSE WAS an all-male, all-black college often described as the Negro Harvard. Years later Martin would talk about the importance of college to his ideological development. Amid the ivy-covered buildings, he would for the first time find the academic freedom to discuss the evils of segregation openly. "We used to sit up way into the morning discussing the social issues of the day," recalls his friend and classmate Walter McCall. "One professor in particular, Walter Shivers, who taught us sociology, constantly brought before us the serious social problems of the day. Particularly, we discussed very seriously at many times the role of leadership in liberating the Negro."

In his first two years at college, Martin debated between embarking upon a career in medicine or in law. He ultimately chose sociology as his major. All the while, he continued to refine his oratorical skills, winning a prize in the Web Oratorical Contest in his sophomore year. He had already decided against following the path of his father and grandfather into the ministry, although the familial pressures in that direction were strong. Like family, church had always been central to Martin's life. It provided not only a religious focus, but a social and intellectual context as well. His was the fundamentalist Baptist church of his father and his grandfather. As a young child, Martin had loved the footstomping gospel songs that caused parishioners to rock with joy. To his mother's accompaniment, he had often led the choir in stirring hymns, such as his favorite "I Want to Be More and More Like Jesus." "One of the things I remember very vividly," recalls Laura Henderson, a long-time member of the Ebenezer congregation, "is he was a great solo singer as a child. He used to sing a lot of solos."

Martin understood the importance of church in the life of the southern black. He knew instinctively that in many ways church was the black man's refuge from the insults and inequities in the white-dominated world. He realized, too, that church provided the black person with a reason to endure this suffering on earth. Since the days of slavery, the promise of heaven and the love of Jesus were frequently all that made survival possible. But as a teenager he had begun to reject the fire and brimstone tradition of his father and grandfather as unintellectual and as irrelevant to the daily life of the oppressed southern black. It is ironic that in later years Roy Wilkins of the NAACP would say in arranging a platform of speakers, "Put King on last. He's in charge of 'rousements.' "

In his early college years, Martin was convinced that he could cause relevant social change more effectively in another profession.

"He and I, being interested in law at the time, thought that this would be the best way in which we could fulfill our life's roles and goals, and thereby help liberate our people," explains McCall.

Events increased Martin's determination to make his mark. During his summer vacation, he traveled with friends from Morehouse to Connecticut to pick tobacco and see the world beyond "Sweet Auburn." In the North for the first time, he and his friends were surprised to find they could enter stores, restaurants, movie theatres, and other public places freely. Here there were no Jim Crow signs prohibiting them or separating them from whites. They were elated. In their youth, they did not readily see the more subtle forms racism took in the North. So for M. L., it was a "bitter pill" when he boarded the train to return home. Forced to sit behind a curtain in the dining car, he felt "as if the curtain had dropped on my selfhood."

While in Connecticut, Martin's friends frequently asked him to lead their devotions. Undoubtedly, these activities caused him to reconsider his decision not to preach. But it was the influence of the distinguished president of Morehouse, Dr. Benjamin E. Mays, that had the greatest impact on Martin's ultimate decision to heed the call to the ministry.

Dr. Mays was a friend of Daddy King and took a special interest in Martin, recognizing his unusual potential. The illustrious preacher-scholar became the young student's "spiritual mentor." According to McCall, "The influence of Dr. Mays upon both of us was tremendous because it was Mays who during those turbulent and very dangerous years fought very relentlessly all forms of segregation."

At Morehouse, King heard sermons and lectures not only by Dr. Mays, but also by other professors, such as his favorite teacher, George D. Kelsey, the head of the religion department. "Many times," recollects McCall, "we would congregate on the corner at Yates and Milton Drugstore upon leaving some of the more profound teachers' classes—like Dr. Ira D. Reed and Walter Shivers and N. P. Tillman. Somehow what these men discussed always had direct bearing upon our thinking patterns."

Melvin Kennedy, his freshman advisor at Morehouse, categorizes Martin as an above-average student, too young still to demonstrate brilliance. He remembers him as "quiet, introspective, and very much introverted; responding whenever called upon and occasionally raising some penetrating questions; yet in different ways showing a strong reaction to many of the subjects that came up in discussion."

These professor-preachers taught a "social gospel" that Martin found intellectually stimulating and socially relevant. Their words appealed to him and helped him develop his own ideas. He began to see that the ministry could be intellectually meaningful, as well as emotionally inspiring. He began to see, too, that the pulpit was the most direct route to his people. The tradition of the southern Baptist preacher-orator was a strong one. Nowhere else did a man have a captive audience so willing to follow where he might lead.

And so it was that in his junior year of college, Martin told his father that he had decided to join the ministry. "We thought he was going to be a lawyer," remembered his father. "He discussed that he was going to be a lawyer, so we looked toward him going on and studying law. When he went to this tobacco farm, they appointed him to lead the devotions for all the students that were there for the summer. So, he started reading scripture and commenting on it, and he just held his colleagues and classmates spellbound when he talked. We didn't know any of this. So the second summer he went back, and they asked him to do the same thing. He was another year older, another year at college, and there he discovered himself." Martin wrote to his mother and said, "You know, Daddy won't believe me, but I'm going to preach."

"I was so glad," said his father, "but I didn't want him to know it. I said, 'M. L., what is this your Mama's telling me you're concerned about preaching? Are you serious about this?'

" 'Yessir, I'm going to preach,' Martin answered.

" 'Don't you know, son, that if you're going to be a lawyer, you'd make money. You won't make any money preaching.'

" 'I'll preach for nothing. I'm not going to worry about money.'

"And he never did! He just would never concern himself about any money-making."

His father arranged a trial sermon in one of the small chapels of the church. "On the night of his sermon," recalled his father, "the church was filled. People stood outside and couldn't get in, so we had to go on up in the sanctuary, and they filled that up. Well, there was nothing to do but go on and license him." Daddy King never really congratulated his son on his success that evening, but later recalled that he went down on his knees that night and thanked the Lord for having given him such a son.

Crozer Theological Seminary, Chester, Pennsylvania

One of those who heard that first sermon was Morehouse's president. "The boy was mature beyond his years," said Dr. Mays. "He spoke as a man who should have had ten years' more experience."

Laura Henderson was a young church member at the time. She remembers the spirit but not the subject of King's first sermon. "Some of us that were quite young then wondered what kind of sermon he was going to preach, and when he finished we were surprised, and pleasantly surprised, because he preached a very good sermon at the very beginning, and we felt that the Lord had laid his hands on him."

"Anybody could see that he was going to make a great preacher just right off to start," boasted his father. "And he began preaching, and it wasn't long before we had ordained him and given him full credentials. This was before he finished college. Each summer when he wasn't in school, he came back and worked with me."

In 1947, when Martin was eighteen years old and a junior in college, he was ordained and made the assistant pastor of Ebenezer Baptist Church. Entering its third generation, the family ministry was now becoming a dynasty. No doubt the young pastor thought he was choosing his own destiny. But to those who knew him, this was the fate to which he was born. His family, his social environment, and his nature all contributed to the decision he now made to become a minister.

In addition to assisting his father, Martin spent his summer vacations from Morehouse working at menial jobs. Engaging in hard physical labor at Railway Express and the Southern Spring Bed Mattress Company, he soon learned a lesson significant to all black laborers: blacks were paid less than whites for equal work. But unlike the majority of his co-workers, Martin was not compelled by economic circumstance to abide the abuses of white bosses. When a foreman at Railway Express persisted in calling him "nigger," he quit the job.

While studying at Morehouse and living at home, Martin dated all the belles of Atlanta's black society. Considering himself something of a Don Juan in those days, he never dated any of them steadily. "He was crazy about dances, and just about the best jitterbug in town," said his brother A. D., who claimed to have a hard time keeping up with his brother socially. Once, after he began assisting his father at Ebenezer, Martin was caught at a local dance, which was an infraction of strict Baptist discipline. His father made him apologize to the congregation from the pulpit the following Sunday.

M. L. graduated from Morehouse at nineteen and received a scholarship to study divinity at Crozer Theological Seminary in Chester, Pennsylvania. One of a half dozen blacks in a student body of one hundred, this was his first experience in an integrated school. He made lasting friendships at Crozer, even among some of the white students. In fact, he was the first black ever to be elected president of the student body.

Crozer was his first real opportunity to live alone, free of his father's sometimes overpowering influence. Classmates remember him as an intensely serious student. He himself remarked that during these years he was forever trying to overcome what he felt was the "Negro stereotype." Concerned that white students would expect him to be tardy, ungroomed, and always wearing a toothy grin, he bent over backward to do the opposite. Walter McCall, who went with King from Morehouse to Crozer, perceived a noticeable change in his friend when he entered the seminary. "He began to take his studies more seriously; he began to take his preaching more seriously. He devoted his time to his books night and day."

At Crozer, the young divinity student studied the psychology of religion, social philosophy, and Christian ethics. He was intellectually mature enough now to assess critically many of the philosophers to whom he had been introduced at Morehouse. He tackled Aristotle, Plato, Hegel, Kant, Rousseau, Martin Luther, John Locke, and Adam Smith. He read Marx's *Communist Manifesto,* concluding that communism was "a Christian heresy." He abhorred its "ethical relativism" and "crippling totalitarianism," believing always that "immoral means cannot bring moral ends." To King, the end could never justify the means. Always, he continued to study the teachings of Jesus.

He read with interest the philosophy of Reinhold Niebuhr, the American theologian who had abandoned the doctrine of pacifism in favor of that of "Christian realism." He also began to develop a particular affinity for Walter Rauschenbusch's philosophy of the "Social Gospel." Increasingly, it became King's conviction "that any religion which professes to be concerned about the souls of men and is not concerned about the social and economic conditions that scar the soul is a spiritually moribund religion."

Unbeknownst to him at the time, one event during his years at Crozer was to influence his future course more directly and more significantly than perhaps any other single incident in his years as a divinity student. In 1949, Dr. Mordecai Johnson, then president of Howard University in Washington, D.C., returned from India and lectured at Fellowship House in Philadelphia. His subject was the life and work of Mahatma Gandhi. This was not King's first exposure to the ideas of the Indian social philosopher. He had heard his Crozer professor George W. Davis lecture on Gandhi, and he had also had the opportunity to hear Dr. A. J. Muste, the noted pacifist and executive secretary of the Fellowship of Reconciliation, talk about Gandhi and his principle of nonviolent resistance. But until now the young King had remained convinced that Gandhi was an impractical idealist.

After hearing Dr. Johnson, himself a rousing orator, King began to be convinced that Gandhi was indeed a great man, who had liberated India from British rule without firing a single shot and had caused political and social change by harnessing the power of love.

"His message," King was to write later, "was so profound and elec-
trifying that I left the meeting and bought a half-dozen books on
Gandhi's life and works."

As King delved deeper into the philosophy of Gandhi, his skep-
ticism concerning the power of love diminished. He began to see
the ethics of Jesus as a powerful instrument for social reform. The
doctrine of Gandhi was not new. At Morehouse, King had read
Henry David Thoreau's essay *On the Duty of Civil Disobedience,*
which had been a source of inspiration to Gandhi. Thoreau's doctrine asserted that no man should cooperate with laws he feels are
unjust, but he must be willing to accept the punishment society sets
for breaking those laws.

In spite of his growing interest, King did not become an immediate convert to Gandhism upon hearing the words of Mordecai
Johnson. He was not convinced Gandhi's tactics could work in
America. Gandhi, after all, had led a *majority* against a *minority*.
The plight of the black American, he felt, was more deeply ingrained
in our society, and the blacks were a frightened and subjugated
minority submerged in a strong and hostile white population. It was
not until the Montgomery bus boycott, when philosophy and action
merged, that King would come to regard passive resistance as a
truly effective weapon and make it his primary tool in the fight against
societal evils.

Even in the ivory tower of Crozer, King was to feel the sting of
those evils personally. Once when he and Walter McCall were on a
double date, a restaurant owner refused to serve the four friends.
When they tried to insist, he threatened them physically. Through
the local NAACP, Martin and Walter tried to take the case to court,
but the suit was dropped when none of the witnesses would testify.

King had straight A's when he graduated from Crozer with a
Bachelor of Divinity in 1951. He was class valedictorian and winner
of the Pearl Plafker Award for the most outstanding student. He
was also awarded the J. Lewis Crozer Fellowship for graduate study.
And, like many middle-class fathers, Daddy King gave him a car in
honor of his graduation.

He decided to enter a doctoral program at Boston University,
where he studied under professors Edgar Sheffield Brightman and
L. Harold DeWolf. Boston University was a center of liberal theology, and the two scholars were renowned proponents of the philosophy of personalism. Both men had a lasting influence on King's
lifelong beliefs in a personal God and in the sacredness of the human

Ebenezer Baptist Church, Atlanta, Georgia.

person. Much later he was to write, "This personal idealism remains today my basic philosophical position. Personalism's insistence that only personality—finite and infinite—is ultimately real, strengthened me in two convictions; it gave me metaphysical and philosophical grounding for the idea of a personal God, and it gave me a metaphysical basis for my belief in the dignity and worth of all human personality."

During this period, however, he was also exposed to the teachings of many great philosophers and proponents of opposing theologies. He took a course on Plato from Dr. Raphael Demos at Harvard. The work of social philosopher Walter Rauschenbusch, *Christianity and the Social Crisis*, continued to provide him with a theological basis for his growing social concern. And while he studied the works of Nietzsche, Hegel, and the existentialists, and wrote his doctoral thesis on Paul Tillich and Henry Nelson Wieman, none was to have the relevance for him that he found in Gandhi.

In Boston, he shared an apartment with Philip Lenud, a friend from Morehouse who was studying divinity at nearby Tufts University. Together they founded the Philosophical Club, where students in the Boston area got together informally to discuss issues and philosophy. Soon what had begun as a group of black men was neither all-black nor all-male.

Martin was gaining a reputation in Boston as a very eligible young bachelor. He and Philip frequented Mrs. Johnson's Western Lunch Box near the university for a home-cooked southern meal. One day, while enjoying his favorite "soul food," he confided to a married friend from Atlanta, "I wish I knew a few girls from down home to go out with. I tell you, these Boston girls are something else. The ones I meet are so reserved."

His friend mentioned a young lady from Alabama, Coretta Scott, who was studying at the New England Conservatory of Music. After much persuasion, she finally gave Martin Coretta's telephone number.

"I am like Napoleon at Waterloo before your charms," he intoned in his deep baritone when he called the first time.

"Why that's absurd," Coretta laughed. "You haven't seen me yet."

A graduate of Antioch College, Coretta Scott was now studying voice in hopes of pursuing a performance career as a soprano. Her father, Obadiah, was a prosperous merchant-landowner from Marion, Alabama. Like Martin's father and grandfather, Obie Scott had determinedly fought racism. He had always taught his family that "if you look a white man in the eyes, he won't harm you."

On their first date Martin took Coretta to lunch between her classes at the conservatory. He was so impressed, not only with her beauty and charm, but also with her intelligence and personality, that he all but proposed on the way home. "You have all the qualities I'm looking for in a wife," he blurted out, even though he hadn't actually been looking for a wife.

"I don't see how you can say that," replied a flabbergasted Coretta. "You don't even know me."

But Martin persisted, "When can I see you again?"

"You may call me later," said Coretta, not knowing exactly what to make of this unusual man. He was nothing like the ministers she had known in the South, and nothing like the men she had been serious about before.

In the months that followed, they spent every spare minute together. She accompanied him to the meetings of the Philosophical Club. They attended concerts and nightclubs and took long walks during which they talked passionately about ideas of all kinds. Martin soon learned that the woman he was in love with opposed racism and segregation as adamantly as he himself.

Coretta's plans did not include marriage to anybody at the moment—least of all a southern Baptist preacher. She wished to continue her voice training and was determined to advance her concert career. "But he was so different from the stereotype I had envisioned," she explained. "He was good—such a very good man." Many people found him intense and serious, but with Coretta, he was playful, fun-loving, and always retained his sense of humor.

Meanwhile, Daddy King had other plans for his son. He wanted Martin to settle down with his childhood sweetheart, the daughter of one of Atlanta's elite black families. But Martin's will prevailed. He and Coretta were married in a fashionable wedding on June 18, 1953, on the spacious lawn of Coretta's father's house. Reverend King, Sr., performed the ceremony, and Martin's brother A. D. was best man.

The couple returned to Boston: Martin to complete the residency requirement for his Ph.D. and Coretta to continue her music education. During this period, Coretta's academic schedule was heavy. Martin, working on his doctoral thesis in their four-room apartment, helped with the household chores and even did some of the cooking. They continued to participate in the Philosophy Club on Friday evenings, and Martin was often invited to preach at nearby churches.

In early 1954, King began looking for a position that would be personally rewarding, while at the same time provide the opportunity to work for black people. All that remained for his doctorate was to complete his dissertation, and in June, Coretta would graduate from the conservatory.

The Kings were considering several positions, both in the North and the South. Martin accepted an offer to preach a trial sermon at the Dexter Avenue Baptist Church in Montgomery, Alabama. The upper-middle-class black church directly across the street from Alabama's statehouse was seeking a minister to replace Dr. Vernon Johns, who had just left. Dr. Johns was well known for his opposition to segregation in Montgomery.

Hoping to make a good impression, King reminded himself before the sermon, "Keep Martin Luther King in the background and God in the foreground and everything will be all right. Remember, you're a channel of the gospel, not a source."

His sermon, entitled "The Three Dimensions of a Complete Life," discussed the strong triangle formed by loving oneself, loving one's neighbor, and loving God. The congregation must have been impressed. King soon received a telegram stating that he had been unanimously chosen as pastor and offering him forty-two hundred dollars, the highest salary of any black minister in Montgomery.

By that time, he had had offers from other churches, in both the North and the South. He had also been offered the deanship at a small college and several teaching positions. Coretta was not enthusiastic about Montgomery. She had grown up only eighty miles away and knew the intense hatred blacks faced in Alabama. More importantly, she knew she would have to abandon her concert career if she and Martin moved south. Knowing that the South would undoubtedly be their ultimate home, she preferred to stay in the North a while longer.

But Martin felt the South was where he was needed and where he could have the greatest impact. He saw Dexter as an opportunity to practice the "social gospel" he had come to believe. Here, too, was an intellectual black congregation that would appreciate his thoughtful oratorical style.

He accepted the offer, and in May he preached his first sermon as the new pastor of the Dexter Avenue Baptist Church. It was the same month that the United States Supreme Court ordered all schools desegregated in the earthshaking *Brown v. Board of Education* decision.

Throughout the summer, the Kings commuted between Boston, Atlanta, and Montgomery. Martin was still completing his thesis and wanted to make as much progress as possible before he began to devote his full time to his new post. By September 1954, Martin and Coretta had moved into the parsonage on South Jackson Street, and on the first Sunday of September, Martin became the full-time pastor of the Dexter Avenue Baptist Church.

The Supreme Court decision had precipitated a growing unrest in Montgomery. But no one, not even Martin, dreamed that the new young minister, fresh out of school, was about to take the lead in a quiet revolution that would change the South irrevocably. Only later would men be reminded of Mordecai's words to Esther in the Old Testament: "Who knows but perhaps thou hast come to the Kingdom for such a time as this."

After hearing the eloquent young minister preach, many in the congregation of Ebenezer Baptist Church felt "the Lord had laid his hands upon him."

Mrs. Rosa Parks, during the Montgomery, Alabama, bus boycott.

Chapter Three

No
Riders
Today

There comes a time when people get tired of being trampled by the iron feet of oppression.

MLK, Jr.

DEXTER AVENUE KING MEMORIAL BAPTIST CHURCH

Organized 1877

The second black Baptist Church in Montgomery. First pastor was Rev. C. O. Boothe. Present structure built 1885. Designed by Pelham J. Anderson: built by William Watkins, a member of the congregation.

Many prominent black citizens of Montgomery have been members. Rev. Martin Luther King, Jr. served as pastor (1954-1960). Montgomery bus boycott organized here December 2, 1955.

ALABAMA HISTORICAL ASSOCIATION   1980

Overleaf: *King's first ministry—the Dexter Avenue Baptist Church.*

MONTGOMERY'S DEXTER AVENUE Baptist Church is a solid brick building located diagonally across the square from Alabama's state capitol, a high-domed classical Georgian structure where, fewer than ninety years before, Alabama had voted to secede from the Union. It was here in Alabama's capital that Jefferson Davis took his oath of office as president of the Confederate States.

Martin Luther King, Jr., had no plan and only the dimmest vision of his future when he took up his post in this "Cradle of the Confederacy." His was a small church with a congregation of only three hundred, compared to four thousand at his father's church in Atlanta. But among the worshippers at Dexter were many of the city's influential black citizens—businessmen, professionals, and many professors from the all-black Alabama State College, Montgomery's only institution of higher learning.

By the spring of 1955, Martin had completed his thesis, and in June, he was awarded his Ph.D. from Boston University. The same month, the United States Supreme Court reaffirmed its 1954 school desegregation decision. In an effort to hasten the process, the Court now added that schools were to be desegregated "with all deliberate speed."

From the beginning of his ministry, King began to implement many new social programs and auxiliary activities at the somewhat conservative church. At the same time, he began to take an interest in the larger community of Montgomery. The least astute observer could see that Montgomery's black citizens were the victims of severe economic depression. Although Montgomery whites boasted of the peaceful racial relations in their city, King quickly saw that peace had been achieved by total submission on the part of blacks.

The Supreme Court's school desegregation decision had had no effect in Montgomery; nor were there any plans now to begin implementing it "with all deliberate speed." In 1955, there were no more than two thousand registered black voters in Montgomery County, although there were nearly thirty thousand blacks of voting age. Not surprisingly, not a single black person held a public office.

Although there were several factions in the black community of Montgomery endeavoring to fight segregation, there was no cohesive leadership. E. D. Nixon, a pullman porter who had long been outspoken against segregation, led a group called the Progressive Democrats, and Rufus Lewis headed the Citizens Committee. There was, as well, a Women's Political Council, led by Mary Fair Burks and Jo Ann Robinson, a member of the faculty at Alabama State

College. But there was a pervasive passivity among Montgomery's black population as a whole and a fragmentation of directions and goals. "People were tired of the humiliating treatment," says Ms. Robinson, "but they lived there; they had homes and jobs. It's not that they were cowards; they were just careful. They were willing to endure terrible humiliation because they had to eat and pay for their homes."

Martin Luther King quickly perceived that the racial peace in Montgomery was superficial and that there was indeed tremendous latent discontent. "One place where the peace had long been precarious," wrote King, "was on the city-wide buses. Here the Negro was daily reminded of the indignities of segregation. There were no Negro drivers, and although some of the white men who drove the buses were courteous, all too many were abusive and vituperative. It was not uncommon to hear them referring to Negro passengers as 'niggers,' 'black cows,' and 'black apes.' "

Black riders were required to pay their fares at the front door, then get off the bus and reboard at the rear. Frequently, a driver would pull away with a black passenger's money before he had time to reach the rear door. The seats in the front of the bus were reserved for white passengers. Blacks could not sit in these seats, even if there were no white passengers on board. If all other seats were occupied, black passengers had to stand, leaving the reserved section empty. If a white person boarded the bus, and there were no seats left in the reserved section, black riders sitting in the seats behind the white section would have to stand up to allow the whites to be seated.

Shortly after King's arrival in Montgomery, a fifteen-year-old schoolgirl was arrested for refusing to give her seat to a white passenger. Although a black citizens committee was formed to meet with officials from the bus company and the city commission, nothing changed. Ultimately, Claudette Colvin was convicted and given a suspended sentence. But her arrest aroused the black community. Long-repressed feelings of resentment were beginning to stir.

This was the atmosphere in Montgomery on December 1, 1955, when Rosa Parks, a seamstress and respected citizen of Montgomery's black community, quietly refused to give her bus seat to a white man. Not even Rosa Parks could fully explain why she decided to keep her seat that day. But whatever the motivation, her courageous act triggered the Montgomery bus boycott, inaugurated the civil rights era, and signaled the end of segregation in the South.

Because she had been the secretary of the local branch of the NAACP, many whites at first believed that Rosa Parks had been planted by that organization to lay the groundwork for a test case in court. In fact, King later wrote, "she was planted there by her personal sense of dignity and self-respect. She was anchored to that seat by the accumulated indignities of days gone by and the boundless aspirations of generations yet unborn. She had been tracked down by the *Zeitgeist*—the spirit of the time."

Rosa Parks still remembers the day as vividly as yesterday. "When I left work that evening and came out of the store I noticed a Cleveland Avenue bus that was quite crowded, so I didn't take that bus. I went across the street to the drugstore and purchased one or two items, because I had a little pain across my neck and shoulders from using the press at work. As I was coming back across the street to the bus stop, I noticed another bus approaching, and I didn't see anybody standing up in the back. But by the time I did get to the bus door, a number of people had gotten on ahead of me, and when I got on the Negro section in the back was well filled, and all of the seats were taken. But there was one vacant seat in the middle section, that part of the bus we could use as long as no white people wanted the seats. The rule was that if the front section filled up and one white person came to sit in the middle section, we would all have to get up and stand in the back. A man was sitting next to the window, so I took a seat next to him.

"On the third stop a few white people boarded the bus, and they took all of the designated white seats, and there was this one man standing. The driver just turned around and he said he needed those front seats, which meant the ones where we were sitting, in order for this man to take a seat. That was segregation.

"The four of us would have to stand up in order to accommodate this one white passenger. When he first spoke, didn't any of us move; but then he spoke a second time with what I would call a threat, because he said, 'You all better make it light on yourselves and let me have those seats.' And at that point the man sitting next to me by the window stood up. The two women stood up and moved out into the aisle. I just moved my legs for him to pass and moved over to the window. The driver looked at me and asked me if I was going to stand up. I told him no, I wasn't. He said, 'If you don't stand up, I'm going to have you arrested.' I told him to go on and have me arrested.

"When the policeman got on the bus, the driver pointed me out and said that he needed the seats. So the policeman approached me and asked me if the driver hadn't asked me to stand. I said, 'Yes.' He asked, 'Why didn't you stand up?' I said I didn't think I should have to. I asked him, 'Why do you push us around?' He said, 'I don't know, but the law is the law, and you are under arrest.' "

E. D. Nixon, the head of the state chapter of the NAACP, was one of the first to learn of the arrest of Rosa Parks. He posted her bail. When word got around to several of the leaders of the Women's Political Council, they suggested that the blacks ought to boycott the buses. Nixon agreed to spearhead the boycott. "We had been laying the groundwork for a boycott for a month before it actually happened," says Ms. Robinson.

Early the next morning, Nixon called Dr. King and Reverend Ralph Abernathy of Montgomery's First Baptist Church and explained the situation. "We have taken this type of thing too long already," he concluded. "I feel that the time has come to boycott the buses. Only through a boycott can we make it clear to the white folks that we will not accept this type of treatment any longer." Both men agreed that a bus boycott would be an effective protest.

The three men began contacting other local ministers and civic leaders, inviting them to a meeting that evening at the Dexter Avenue Baptist Church. There they presented the proposal that the black citizens of Montgomery should boycott the buses on the following Monday. Not a single person questioned the validity or desirability of the boycott, and they soon began to address themselves to the logistics of how it could be effectively achieved. The ministers promised to go to their congregations on Sunday morning and heartily endorse the one-day protest on Monday, December 5. Committees were appointed and a citywide mass meeting was planned for Monday evening to decide how long the boycott should continue. One committee prepared a leaflet to be distributed on Saturday. It read:

Don't ride the bus to work, to town, to school, or any place Monday, December 5.

Another Negro woman has been arrested and put in jail because she refused to give up her bus seat.

Don't ride the buses to work, to town, to school, or anywhere on Monday. If you work, take a cab, or share a ride, or walk.

Come to a mass meeting, Monday at 7:00 P.M., at the Holt Street Baptist Church for further instruction.

Another committee contacted all the black taxicab companies and asked them to transport protestors in their 210 taxis and charge only the ten-cent bus fare. Every black-owned taxi company agreed to participate in the protest.

On Saturday morning, some unexpected publicity helped spread the word of the boycott. The *Montgomery Advertiser* had gotten hold of a copy of the leaflet from a white employer and printed the story on the front page.

On Monday, Martin and Coretta rose early, eager to see what was going to happen. They had calculated that 60 percent cooperation by the black community would be considered successful. As the first bus passed the stop in front of the King home, Coretta cried, "Martin, Martin, come quickly!" As he ran to the window, Coretta pointed and said, "Darling, it's empty!" Fifteen minutes later a second bus passed. It, too, was empty. And when the third came along a little later, it carried only two white passengers.

Jumping into his car, King cruised all the major streets and examined the passing buses. He couldn't believe it—hardly a single black rider. People were hitchhiking, sharing rides, walking—sometimes as far as twelve miles. But they stayed off the buses.

Spectators gathered at some of the bus stops and cheered as the empty buses pulled away. Youngsters called out, "No riders today!" Motorcycle policemen were assigned to follow the buses through the black neighborhoods to ensure that anyone who wanted to ride the bus was not prevented from doing so. But no one wanted to ride. Even though the police were looking for trouble, they made only one arrest that day—a college student who was helping an elderly black lady cross the street was charged with "intimidating passengers."

Rosa Parks's trial was also scheduled for Monday. She was found guilty and fined fourteen dollars for disobeying the segregation law. This, too, turned out to be extremely positive for the movement. It was one of the first clear-cut instances of a black person being convicted for violating a segregation law. In the past, most of the cases had been dismissed, or the offender had been charged with disorderly conduct. Now Rosa Parks would be able to appeal her case and challenge the constitutionality of the segregation laws.

At a meeting Monday afternoon, the leaders of the protest decided

Reverend Ralph Abernathy, minister of Montgomery's First Baptist Church, became King's lifelong friend and confidant.

to create a formal organization to determine how to capitalize on their success and how to proceed. After a great deal of discussion about the name of this new organization, Ralph Abernathy came up with the Montgomery Improvement Association (MIA). Martin King was elected president. King's ability was already evident, and as a relative newcomer to Montgomery, he was not a member of any of the political factions. "He had no friends to reward and no enemies to punish," explained Rev. T. J. Jimerson, a longtime friend of the King family who lived in nearby Selma. "He was not a part of any system even among blacks in the community of Montgomery. He was a neutral person, so I think he was ideally situated to lead. Of course, history now records for all of us that he was divinely inspired for it."

The newly organized group began by discussing plans for the evening mass meeting. Some in the group felt it was important to keep their actions a secret from the press. Some feared reprisals and did not want it known who their leaders were. E. D. Nixon spoke up and said, "We are acting like little boys. Somebody's name will have to be known, and if we are afraid we might just as well fold up right now. We must also be men enough to discuss our recommendations in the open; this idea of secretly passing something around on a paper is a lot of bunk. The white folks are eventually going to find out about it anyway. We'd better decide now if we are going to be fearless men or scared boys."

Moved by his words, the rest of the group agreed. They further agreed that the protest should continue until their demands were met. Reverend Abernathy was to head a committee that would draw up a resolution to be approved at the mass meeting that evening.

As early as 5:00 P.M., people began to pack the church in anticipation of the 7:00 meeting. Television cameras and reporters were present when the meeting began with a mighty chorus of "Onward, Christian Soldiers." The crowd cheered as Rosa Parks told her story. She was their courageous heroine. But it was King's speech that characterized the mood of the crowd. He told them the story of Rosa Parks's ordeal. And then he proclaimed:

"There comes a time when people get tired of being trampled over by the iron feet of oppression. There comes a time, my friends, when people get tired of being flung across the abyss of humiliation where they experience the bleakness of nagging despair. There comes a time when people get tired of being pushed out of the glittering sunlight of life's July, and left standing amidst the piercing chill of

Montgomery's blacks refused to ride the buses, willingly substituting "tired feet for tired souls."

an Alpine November. We are here this evening because we're tired now." He was a Baptist minister, and they were his congregation. They applauded him and responded with the encouraging words that were a traditional part of the Sunday morning sermon.

"Now let us say that we are not here advocating violence," he insisted as he continued. "We have overcome that. I want it to be known throughout Montgomery and throughout this nation that we are Christian people. . . . The only weapon that we have in our hands this evening is the weapon of protest."

"My friends," he continued amidst their cheers, "I want it to be known that we're going to work with grim and firm determination to gain justice on the buses in this city. And we are not wrong, we are not wrong in what we are doing. If we are wrong, then the Supreme Court of this nation is wrong. If we are wrong, the Constitution of the United States is wrong. If we are wrong, God Almighty is wrong."

Four thousand people applauded wildly. Martin Luther King had found his true calling.

"This was the time that the people were brought face to face with the type of man that Martin Luther [King] was," said Rufus Lewis. "Not only the people who came to the mass meeting, but those who nominated him, too. That was the great awakening. It was astonishing, the man spoke with so much force."

Next Reverend Abernathy took the podium and explained the resolution that was to be presented to the bus company and city officials. They were proposing a three-point plan:

1) passengers were to be guaranteed courteous treatment by bus operators;
2) passengers were to be seated on a first come, first served basis, with blacks sitting from the back of the bus forward, and whites from the front back;
3) black operators were to be employed on predominantly black routes.

When Abernathy asked all those in favor of the proposal to stand, the entire crowd rose and cheered. They unanimously decided to stay off the buses until all of their demands were met. With that vote, Montgomery was thrust into history. This was the beginning of the nonviolent civil rights movement.

The leaders realized emotional fervor had carried the protest to this point. They knew, too, that if it were to continue as a successful movement, it would need considerable organization. So the following day, committees began planning the logistics that would enable 17,500 bus riders to stay off the buses. The first priority was to organize an effective, dependable system of transportation. The arrangement with the taxicab companies had to be a temporary one. Within four days, the city invoked its minimum fare ordinance, prohibiting black taxi drivers from offering below standard fares.

But by Tuesday, December 13—eight days after the protest began—a car-pool system was functioning with military precision. Black car owners from all walks of life volunteered to drive former bus riders to and from their jobs. They were joined by sympathetic white and black airmen from the nearby airbase.

Many white housewives picked up their black domestic workers, rather than be deprived of their services. One white matron asked her maid, "Isn't this bus boycott terrible?" As they both were the product of two hundred years of southern tradition, she no doubt expected a positive response, but perhaps not the one she got.

The old black matriarch replied, "Yes, ma'am, it sure is. And I just told all my young'uns that this kind of thing is white folks' business and we just stay off the buses till they get this whole thing settled."

Dispatch and pick-up stations were set up throughout the city. But many people preferred to walk, seeing it as a symbolic gesture. When one driver stopped to pick up an elderly black woman, who was walking with obvious difficulty, she waved him on, saying, "I'm not walking for myself. I'm walking for my children and my grandchildren."

At first, officials from the bus company and the city made no move to open discussions with the black community. They were convinced the protest would fizzle with the first rainy day. But when the first rainy day came, and the buses remained empty, the officials sent word that they were willing to negotiate.

King was chosen to serve as the MIA's spokesman, and he was to present the same three proposals that had been agreed upon at the Monday night meeting. The resolution was extremely conservative, so much so that black leaders in other cities were disappointed and felt that the MIA should demand more. "I sent them a telegram," remembers Dr. Joseph Lowery, third president of the

Southern Christian Leadership Conference (SCLC) and then a minister in Mobile, Alabama. "It said, 'You guys must be crazy. We already have that arrangement in Mobile. We want everybody to be able to sit everywhere.' "

Nevertheless, the mayor and the city commissioners, spurred by Jack Crenshaw, the attorney for the bus company, challenged the legality of the seating proposal, contending that it would be a violation of the law. In the presence of reporters and television cameras, the white officials were intransigent. The only demand to which they were willing to agree was that requesting courtesy on the part of drivers, even though the other demands did not threaten the basic segregation laws and had already been adopted in other cities of the South, such as Atlanta, Nashville, and Mobile.

But King understood the depth of the problem when Crenshaw betrayed his real concerns: "If we granted the Negroes these demands, they would go about boasting of a victory that they had won over the white people; and this we will not stand for."

In the meetings that followed, neither side budged. Meanwhile, the black leaders learned that the Montgomery bus company was owned by the National City Lines, Inc., which was headquartered in Chicago and operated bus companies in thirty-five cities. They reasoned that if they could negotiate with the officers of that company, who were not southerners raised with segregation, perhaps they could make some progress. They wired the president of the company, asking him to come to Montgomery immediately or send a representative to negotiate. There was renewed optimism when they received a reply that one of the company's vice-presidents would arrive in Montgomery in several days. But the days came and went and there was no word from the bus company.

On December 15, King received a call from a white friend and supporter, saying that he had heard that an executive from the National City Lines had been in town for several days. The bus official made no effort to speak with any representative of the Montgomery Improvement Association, even though it was they who had invited him. Eventually, the mayor sent word that he was calling a citizens committee to meet with bus officials and black leaders on the morning of December 17. The executive board of the MIA met and agreed to stand firm on the three proposals.

When they arrived for the meeting, King noticed an unfamiliar face entering the room with the attorneys from the bus company. He was introduced as C. K. Totten of Chicago. King also recognized several black delegates who were not on the committee appointed by the black community to represent them. He soon learned they were there at the invitation of Mayor W. A. Gayle.

When the meeting was called to order, King was asked to explain the MIA's proposals. When he was finished, C. K. Totten, representing the National City Lines, rose to give his response. It was immediately clear that he had been "brainwashed" by the city commissioners and local bus officials with whom he had spent the last three days. King was furious. Unable to restrain himself, he said, "Mr. Totten has not been fair in his assertions. He has made a statement that is completely biased. In spite of the fact that he was asked to Montgomery by the MIA, he has not done the Negro community the simple courtesy of hearing their grievances. The least that all of us can do in our deliberations is to be honest and fair."

After several of the citizens who had been invited by the mayor had spoken, the mayor announced that he would appoint a small group from the citizens committee to continue negotiating with representatives from the bus company and the MIA. The group was to work out a settlement and bring a recommendation back to him. Although he attempted to stack the committee with whites and his two handpicked black delegates, Jo Ann Robinson of the Women's Political Council took issue. She insisted the only fair way to handle the problem was to appoint an equal number of blacks and whites. Reluctantly, the mayor did so.

When the new committee came to order, several suggestions were made that would have undercut the blacks' demands, and no agreement could be reached. Several of the white members then suggested that the blacks return to the buses and that the committee return after the Christmas holidays to work out a settlement. Once again, the response of the black leaders was negative. They knew their efforts would have been in vain if they called off the protest with only the promise that something might be done later. The group adjourned, agreeing to reassemble on Monday morning.

As they left the meeting, King had his first opportunity to talk directly to Totten. The bus executive admitted that the plan they were recommending was being followed in Mobile, where the bus company was also owned by National City Lines, Inc. "As far as I'm concerned," Totten admitted, "it would work very well in Montgomery. But the commission seems to feel that it will not be acceptable."

Meanwhile the protest continued. Letters of support and contributions had begun to pour in from all over the world to help defray the costs of the boycott. Eventually, these funds would enable MIA to buy a fleet of fifteen station wagons. Each was emblazoned with the name of a different church, and these cars became the core of the transportation system.

To King fell the most difficult task of keeping the people emotionally involved and enthusiastic despite whatever setbacks befell the protest. As the negotiations continued to flounder, this became difficult indeed. "Had he not been there, many people might have gone back to the buses," says Ms. Robinson. "He showed them that walking hadn't ever killed anybody. That it was a matter of being human beings." King liked to use as an example the story of Old Mother Pollard, who refused the rides proffered by carpoolers, saying, "My feet is tired, but my soul is rested."

The leaders endeavored constantly to disseminate the philosophy of nonviolence through regular mass meetings that were held on a rotating basis in the various black churches. At first these meetings were held twice a week and eventually reduced to once a week. The churches were an indispensable channel of communication.

Although the basic philosophy that guided the movement ultimately came to be called passive or nonviolent resistance, these terms came later. In the early days of the boycott, King and the other leaders preached the gospel of "Christian love." It was initially the Sermon on the Mount that motivated the black people of Montgomery to social action.

Only later did the inspiration of Mahatma Gandhi exert its influence. In fact, the first mention of Gandhi appeared in a letter to the editor in the *Montgomery Advertiser*. It was written by Juliette Morgan, a white librarian. "The Negroes of Montgomery seem to have taken a lesson from Gandhi—and our own Thoreau, who influenced Gandhi," she wrote. "Their own task is greater than Gandhi's, however, for they have greater prejudice to overcome. One feels that history is being made in Montgomery these days, the most important in her career. It is hard to imagine a soul so dead, a heart so hard, a vision so blinded and provincial as not to be moved with admiration at the quiet dignity, discipline and dedication with which the Negroes have conducted their boycott."

King had also begun to think of the protest as "an act of massive noncooperation"—civil disobedience in the style of Henry David Thoreau. Regardless of the label, the philosophy was one of nonviolence. Every speaker at every meeting was urged to make nonviolence a central theme in his remarks. In his own speeches, King stressed that the use of violence in their struggle would be both impractical and immoral. Hate must be met with love; violence with nonviolence; physical force with soul force.

It became increasingly imperative that this philosophy continue to be expounded, for as the city officials saw the determination and unity of the black community, they began to resort to other means to undermine the boycott. At one point, in an effort to persuade black riders to return to the buses, the city council planted a false story that a settlement had been reached. Later, they attempted to turn blacks against their leaders by spreading a rumor concerning the misuse of MIA funds.

In another effort to divide the black community and set the people at odds with their leaders, the city commissioners publicly joined forces with the segregationist White Citizens Council. They initiated a "get tough" policy that included threatening car-pool drivers with loss of insurance and licenses and charging waiting riders with vagrancy. "One of the main problems," said boycott organizer Rufus Lewis, "was the police department intimidating and harrassing and arresting the drivers that they knew were picking up people to take to work. They were giving tickets for blocking the traffic, giving tickets for speeding, giving tickets for almost anything."

King himself was arrested, in what was to be the first of many civil disobedience arrests, for allegedly going thirty miles per hour in a twenty-five mile per hour zone. He was taken to jail, and while his good friend Ralph Abernathy went to raise the necessary cash bond to release him, a number of King's friends and parishioners assembled in front of the jail. Soon the crowd was so large that the jailor panicked and released King on his own bond.

When even the "get tough" policy failed to dissuade the protestors, the White Citizens Council turned to more dramatic means. From the first days of the boycott, the Kings had been receiving threatening calls and letters. These increased as time went on, until by mid-January, they were receiving as many as thirty to forty threats a day.

On January 30, the threats turned to violence. King had gone to attend the regular Monday mass meeting at the First Baptist Church. Coretta was at home with their baby daughter, Yolanda Denise. The Kings' first child had been born just two weeks before the protest began. Mrs. Mary Lucy Williams, a member of the Dexter Avenue congregation, had come to the house to keep Coretta company

in her husband's absence. At about 9:30, while watching television, the two women heard a noise that sounded as if someone had thrown a brick at the front of the house. In a matter of seconds, an explosion rocked the house. A bomb had gone off on the front porch.

The explosion was heard many blocks away, and word soon spread to the mass meeting. From the speaker's platform, King saw an usher give a message to Abernathy, and judging from the worried glances, he soon determined that whatever had happened concerned him. He called Ralph over and asked him what was the matter. Hesitantly, Abernathy said, "Your house has been bombed." When King asked about his wife and child, Abernathy told him they were still checking. Before leaving the church, King urged the congregation to adhere strictly to their philosophy of nonviolence. "Let us keep moving," he preached, "with the faith that what we are doing is right, and with the even greater faith that God is with us in the struggle."

When King reached his home, an angry mob stood outside his house. The police, who were trying brusquely to clear the area, were being ignored. King saw immediately that many people were armed, and he heard one black man say to a policeman, "I ain't gonna move nowhere. That's the trouble now; you white folks is always pushin' us around. Now you got your .38 and I got mine; so let's battle it out."

King rushed into the house to learn that Coretta and nine-week-old Yoki were safe. Fortunately, when Coretta and Mrs. Williams had heard the thud, they had run to the back of the house. Had they gone to the porch to investigate, they might have been killed.

Mayor Gayle and Police Commissioner Clyde Sellers had reached the King home by this time. When they expressed their regrets that this had happened in "our city," one of the trustees of Dr. King's church who was standing nearby said, "You may express your regrets, but you must face the fact that your public statements created the atmosphere for this bombing. This is the end result of your 'get-tough' policy." Neither the mayor nor the commissioner replied.

By this time, the crowd outside was quite angry and unpredictable. The police were unable to disperse them. King himself walked to the front porch and asked for the crowd's attention. Instantly, there was complete silence. King assured the mob that he and his family were safe. Then he continued, "If you have weapons, take them home; if you do not have them, please do not seek to get them. We cannot solve this problem through retaliatory violence.

Regular mass meetings were held to spread the philosophy of nonviolence.

We must meet violence with nonviolence." Urging them to leave peacefully, he reminded them of the words of Jesus, "Love your enemies; bless them that curse you; pray for them that despitefully use you." He concluded with words that brought tears to many eyes in the crowd, "Remember, if I am stopped, this movement will not stop, because God is with this movement. Go home with this glowing faith and this radiant assurance."

There were shouts of "Amen" and "God bless you." King then had to silence the jeering crowd when the police commissioner rose to address them. He offered a reward to anyone who could identify the offenders, and the crowd then began to disperse. What verged on becoming a night of terror and rioting ended in a magnificent demonstration of the power of nonviolence.

Two nights later, a stick of dynamite was thrown on E. D. Nixon's lawn. Although no one was hurt, a large crowd once again gathered. But this time, too, peace prevailed, and nonviolence won yet another test.

On February 1, the Montgomery Improvement Association filed suit in U.S. Federal District Court asking that segregation on buses be abolished on the grounds that it violated the Fourteenth Amendment to the United States Constitution. The hearing was scheduled for May 11.

Finding that even terror tactics had not dissuaded the protestors, the city invoked an old state law against boycotting and indicted more than one hundred blacks, including King and twenty-three other ministers. When word came on February 21 that the arrests were to begin the next day, King was out-of-town. Against the wishes of his father and many family friends, he resolved to return immediately to Montgomery to turn himself in.

When he arrived, Abernathy told him that people had rushed to the jail to get arrested the day before. No one was afraid. No one had tried to resist arrest. What King found when he reached the jail was an almost jovial atmosphere. King saw confidence, where once there had been fear; pride, where there had been humiliation.

When the trial began on March 19, King was called as the first defendant. Twenty-eight witnesses were brought to the stand by the defense. Fearlessly, with courage and dignity, they told their personal stories of abuse on Montgomery's buses. The tales were of humiliation, of injury, even of death. Nevertheless, after nearly four days of testimony, Judge Eugene Carter found King guilty of violating the state's antiboycott law and sentenced him to pay a five hundred–dollar fine or serve 386 days of hard labor. His attorneys immediately moved to appeal. Judge Carter entered a continuance on the other cases until King's appeal was complete.

With King's conviction, the movement was stronger than ever. Every black person in Montgomery felt he, too, had been convicted with King. If there was concern that the movement might falter, this was all that was needed to keep the blacks off the buses. When King walked out of the courthouse, hundreds of spectators, black and white, began to sing, "We ain't gonna ride the buses no more."

The arrests and trial had drawn national attention. An editorial in a Hartford, Connecticut, newspaper wrote prophetically: "Emerging from the racial conflict in Montgomery, Alabama, is the growing leadership of a Negro clergyman, Martin Luther King. By virtue of his intelligence and piety Mr. King has gradually become the spokesman for passive resistance. It is well to remember his name. For if this movement is successful, as it appears likely, the Reverend Dr. King will become not only a national hero among his race, but the continuing spearhead in the fight against segregation."

In early June, the U.S. District Court found the city bus segregation laws of Alabama unconstitutional. Even though the attorneys for the city of Montgomery appealed the case to the Supreme Court of the United States, victory now seemed only a matter of time. And Montgomery's buses remained empty.

In the early fall, the city launched a new attack—this time on the car-pool system, calling it a public nuisance. At the same time, the companies that held the car insurance policies decided to refuse to insure the MIA station wagons. Once again, the protestors found themselves in court. The night before, at a mass meeting, King had urged those present not to lose faith. But he later admitted that at that moment his own optimism was faltering. After they had suffered for nearly a year, could he now ask them to walk to and from their jobs every day?

"This may well be," he said, "the darkest hour just before dawn. We have moved all of these months with the daring faith that God was with us in our struggle. The many experiences of days gone by have vindicated that faith in a most unexpected manner. We must go out with the same faith, the same conviction. We must believe that a way will be made out of no way."

In spite of his hopeful prayer, there was an overwhelming pessimism in the room that night.

Chapter Four

A
New
Sense
of
Dignity

*When the history books of the future are
written, they will say there was a great people
in Montgomery who did what had to be done, who
did what was right, and from this moment on
there can be no turning back.*

MLK, Jr.

IN JUDGE CARTER'S court the following day, November 13, 1956, the city of Montgomery sought a temporary injunction to halt the car pool. King was certain that without the car pool the boycott could not continue. In despair, he listened to the proceedings. The city's attorneys were also asking for fifteen thousand dollars in compensation for money lost as a result of the bus ban. "The clock said it was noon," he later recalled, "but it was midnight in my soul."

Just before the luncheon recess, there was a sudden commotion in the courtroom. A reporter showed something to Mayor Gayle and Commissioner Sellers, who both jumped up and left the court. Rex Thomas, from the Associated Press, handed Dr. King a slip of paper. "Here is the decision you've been waiting for," he said. "Read this release." The AP wire read: "The United States Supreme Court today affirmed a decision of a special three-judge U.S. District Court in declaring Alabama's state and local laws requiring segregation on buses unconstitutional."

"God Almighty has spoken from Washington, D.C.," cried one jubilant bystander.

Predictably, Judge Carter granted the city a temporary injunction to halt the car pool. But his decision was an ironic anticlimax. For on the same day the local court banned the car pool, the United States Supreme Court eliminated the conditions that had made it necessary.

News of their victory spread quickly. Two simultaneous mass meetings were scheduled for the next day. Eight thousand people crowded into the two churches where the leaders recommended that the protest be ended immediately, but that the return to the buses be delayed until the official mandate arrived from Washington in a few days. The congregation both wept and cheered that evening when Reverend Robert Graetz, the only white minister in the leadership of the movement, read the scripture according to Paul: "When I was a child, I spoke as a child, I understood as a child, I thought as a child, but when I became a man, I put away childish things." All those present recognized how far they had come, how much they had grown—and how far they had still to go.

Forty carloads of white-hooded Ku Klux Klansmen rode through Montgomery that night. But on this evening, black people didn't hide in dark houses behind locked doors, fearing death. With their lights on and doors open, they acted as if they were watching a parade. A few even waved at the passing cars. The courage this took was one more testimony to the faith they had acquired through their long year of struggle.

King soon learned that it would be nearly a month before the mandate arrived from the Supreme Court. In the meantime, the car-pool system had been prohibited. Quickly, a voluntary share-a-ride plan was created. Montgomery's buses remained empty.

The mass meetings also continued. Their purpose now was to prepare people for integrated buses. Nonviolence remained the central theme. "We must not take this as a victory over the white man," the leaders reiterated, "but as a victory for justice and democracy." There were training sessions in nonviolent techniques, where through role-playing people learned how to respond to whatever behavior might confront them.

The leaders went into schools urging students to accept their victory gracefully, with dignity, and to adhere to the principles of nonviolence. A list of suggestions for integrated buses was distributed. The flyer urged blacks to accept their new responsibility with "a calm and loving dignity," and encouraged the reader to memorize the seventeen general and specific suggestions, "so that our nonviolent determination may not be endangered." The suggestions ranged from "Pray for guidance and commit yourself to complete nonviolence in word and action as you enter the bus" to "Do not deliberately sit by a white person, unless there is no other seat." The final admonition read: "If you feel you cannot take it, walk for another week or two. We have confidence in our people. GOD BLESS YOU ALL."

Unfortunately, no one undertook the responsibility of preparing Montgomery's white community for integration. On the contrary, the White Citizens Council took the lead, threatening, "Any attempt to enforce this decision will lead to riot and bloodshed."

On December 18, the city commissioners issued a statement that read in part: "The City Commission will not yield one inch, but will do all in its power to oppose the integration of the Negro race with the white race in Montgomery, and will forever stand like a rock against social equality, inter-marriage, and mixing of the races under God's creation and plan."

When the bus integration order finally reached Montgomery on December 20, 1956, more than a year after Rosa Parks refused to give up her seat on the bus, King spoke to an overflow crowd at the evening's mass meeting: "This is the time that we must evince calm dignity and wise restraint. Emotions must not run wild. Violence must not come from any of us, for if we become victimized with

After the United States Supreme Court mandated integration of Montgomery's buses, a reign of violence led by the Ku Klux Klan and other racist groups ensued.

violent intents, we will have walked in vain, and our twelve months of glorious dignity will be transformed into an eve of gloomy catastrophe. . . . It is my firm conviction that God is working in Montgomery. Let all men of goodwill, both Negro and white, continue to work with Him. With this dedication we will be able to emerge from the bleak and desolate midnight of man's inhumanity to man to the bright and glittering daybreak of freedom and justice."

The following morning, King, along with Abernathy, E. D. Nixon, Rosa Parks, and Glenn Smiley, one of the few southern white ministers who actively supported the boycott, rode the first integrated bus in Montgomery. There were no incidents of violence and only a few relatively minor episodes of hostility reported the first day. Even the *Montgomery Advertiser* wrote: "The calm but cautious acceptance of this significant change in Montgomery's way of life came without any major disturbance."

But the peace was short-lived. Within a week, buses were being fired upon; a black teenage girl was beaten by a group of white men; a pregnant black women was shot in the leg. Unbridled, the White Citizens Council and the KKK led the violence. A reign of terror had begun.

The segregationists began a slur campaign against Martin Luther King. They attempted to turn his people against him by distributing leaflets that were allegedly written by dissatisfied blacks. "We get shot at while he rides," the flyers read. "He is getting us in more trouble every day. Wake up. Run him out of town." But almost everyone knew the true source of these defamations was the white racists.

By Christmas, bus protests had begun in several other southern cities. Bayard Rustin, a leader of the Fellowship of Reconciliation (FOR)—a long-established pacifist group—approached King with the idea of setting up a permanent organization that would give voice to this growing movement. They agreed that the black church should be the core of the new organization because it offered ready-made leadership and was by far the most encompassing and effective institution in the black community.

On January 9, 1957, King and Abernathy traveled to Atlanta, where King had called a meeting of black leaders from all over the South for the following day. More than sixty black ministers, committed to a southern movement, had responded to his call. They formed the nucleus of what would become the Southern Christian Leadership Conference.

When a long-distance telephone call from Abernathy's wife, Juanita, awakened them at 2:00 A.M., King knew it must be serious. He soon learned that the Abernathys' home had been bombed. Fortunately, the wife and daughter of his dearest friend were safe. Before Abernathy could finish relating the details, Juanita called a second time and told them that Abernathy's First Baptist Church had also been bombed and that there had been several other bombings as well. The two ministers rushed back to Montgomery to learn that three other Baptist churches had been bombed, along with the home of white minister Bob Graetz.

Even many of Montgomery's white citizens were outraged by the bombings. No matter how committed they might be to segregation, they were on the side of law and order, and they would not condone violence and anarchy. A two thousand–dollar award was offered for the arrests of suspects, and many of the city's most influential citizens went on record condemning the bombings.

That afternoon King returned to Atlanta, wanting at least to make an appearance at the meeting of black leaders, which he had initiated. The group included such prominent activist ministers as Reverend Fred Shuttlesworth of Birmingham, Reverend C. K. Steele of Tallahassee, and Reverend Joseph Lowery of Mobile. Each of these men had organized and led protests in his own city. Now there was general agreement that they should meet the following month to form a permanent organization through which they could coordinate and expand the movement across the South.

King returned from that first meeting in Atlanta to find all bus service in Montgomery discontinued. Feeling personally guilty about the bombings and discouraged by this fruitless outcome of many months of struggle, King was terribly depressed when he addressed the mass meeting on January 15, his twenty-eighth birthday. For the first time in the thirteen months of the boycott, he nearly broke down in public. Seized by emotion that he could not control, he prayed, "Lord, I hope no one will have to die as a result of our struggle for freedom in Montgomery. Certainly I don't want to die. But if anyone has to die, let it be me."

"No, no," the audience shouted wildly. Unable to continue, but feeling tremendous relief, King allowed himself to be led from the pulpit.

The violence gradually subsided in Montgomery, but not before a second wave of bombings shook the city. This time, the Kings found a bundle of smoldering dynamite on their own front porch.

King responded with prophetic fatalism: "Tell Montgomery that they can keep shooting and I'm going to stand up to them; tell Montgomery they can keep bombing and I'm gong to stand up to them. If I had to die tomorrow morning I would die happy because I've been to the Mountaintop and I've seen the Promised Land, and it's going to be here in Montgomery."

Eventually, seven white men were arrested for the bombings. In spite of all the evidence, including signed confessions, they were never convicted. But the violence came to an end, and desegregation began to proceed smoothly on Montgomery's buses.

With the success of the Montgomery bus boycott, King declared that a "new Negro" had been born in the South. He himself was catapulted to prominence. *Jet* magazine hailed him as "a symbol of divinely inspired hope," "a kind of modern Moses who has brought new self-respect to Southern Negroes." In February, he was featured on the cover of *Time*. "King," according to the newsweekly, "reached beyond lawbooks and writs, beyond violence and threats, to win his people—and challenge all people—with a spiritual force that aspired even to ending prejudice in man's mind." The magazine continued, "He struck where an attack was least expected, and where it hurt most: at the South's Christian conscience." The article quoted one white minister, who said, "I know of very few white Southern ministers who aren't troubled and don't have admiration for King. They've become tortured souls."

King emerged from the boycott a national leader with a popular backing rivaling Booker T. Washington's at the turn of the century. The Southern Christian Leadership Conference (SCLC) would be, in the words of its third president, Dr. Joseph Lowery, "the vehicle . . . the chair that Martin rode and drove through the turbulence of the late fifties and sixties." The SCLC met formally for the first time in New Orleans on February 14, 1957. Fresh from his victory in Montgomery, King had proven himself a charismatic leader. He was unanimously elected president of the new organization.

"Dr. King saw a need for an organization of this kind," recollects Reverend T. J. Jimerson of Baton Rouge, "and we all concurred. We felt that there was a need, with the changing times in the South and with the injustices that had been perpetrated upon blacks from the very beginning. We had been leaders in our respective communities and we had been working closely with him, so we just tied our strengths together, and Dr. Martin Luther King was elected the first President. He served until his death.

King was unanimously elected president of the Southern Christian Leadership Conference. The newly formed organization held its first staff meetings in an Atlanta restaurant.

Dr. Joseph E. Lowery, third president of the SCLC, was among the founding members of the organization.

"Primarily, in the beginning, all of the people in the SCLC were ministers. We called it a Southern Christian Leadership Conference because of the attachment that the church had by all of us being ministers. We didn't call it a Pastors Conference because we wanted within our membership laymen, and certainly we felt that there was a place in the organization for both men and women who were not members of the clergy."

Its founders perceived the SCLC as an extension of their ministry. "I think that properly reviewed and evaluated, the SCLC from then till now will be seen as the cutting edge, the moral voice, the prophetic outcry, the independent force in the struggle," says Lowery.

The new organization would consist entirely of local affiliates, each of which would send five voting delegates to the SCLC conventions, which were originally held twice a year and eventually annually. The affiliates would work with the black churches to coordinate local civil rights activities.

Both the goals and the methods of the SCLC differed from those of existing Negro organizations. The National Urban League, for example, worked almost exclusively in the North. Congress of Racial Equality (CORE) had been using Gandhian direct action techniques since as early as 1942, but it had not been active in the South and by 1957 had no effective field staff. The NAACP concentrated its efforts on legal battles and was beginning to achieve successes in this arena, most notably in the *Brown v. Board of Education* school desegregation decision. The SCLC alone aimed to use the Montgomery method to create a grassroots freedom movement in Dixie. They would use "spiritual strategy" to support the NAACP's legal strategy.

A number of years later, Dr. King articulated five fundamental goals of the SCLC. These had evolved over the course of his major campaigns in the South. "First, to stimulate nonviolent, direct mass action to expose and remove the barriers of segregation and discrimination; second to disseminate the creative philosophy and techniques of nonviolence through local and area workshops; third to secure the right and unhampered use of the ballot for every citizen; fourth to achieve full citizenship rights, and the total integration of the Negro into America life; and fifth, to reduce the cultural lag through our citizenship training program." [handwritten: spread around]

At their preliminary organizational meeting in Atlanta, the nascent SCLC drafted an appeal to President Dwight Eisenhower and Vice-President Richard Nixon to "come South immediately to make a major speech in a major Southern city urging all Southerners to accept and abide by the Supreme Court's decision as the law of the land." They received polite refusals.

At their next meeting in New Orleans, they asked the president to call a White House conference on civil rights, and they put the chief executive on notice that if "remedial steps" were not taken, the SCLC would be obliged "to initiate a mighty Prayer Pilgrimage to Washington." When they received word from the White House that the "moment is unpropitious," King joined with Roy Wilkins, the executive secretary of the NAACP, and A. Philip Randolph, the head of the Brotherhood of Sleeping Car Porters (at that time the strongest Negro union in America), to begin planning the Prayer Pilgrimage.

Chapter Five

A
Symbol
of
Hope

*Do your work so well that no one could
do it better. Do it so well that all the
hosts of heaven and earth will have to say:
Here lived a man who did his job as if
God Almighty called him at this particular
time in history to do it.*

MLK, Jr.

ON MAY 17, 1957, three years to the day after the Supreme Court's epochal school desegregation decision, thirty-seven thousand marchers stood before the Lincoln Memorial in the largest civil rights demonstration yet organized. Even in the company of black leaders such as Randolph, Wilkins, and Adam Clayton Powell and celebrities such as Jackie Robinson, Mahalia Jackson, Sammy Davis, Jr., and Harry Belafonte, King was the undisputed hero of the day.

His first truly national address firmly established his position as foremost black leader of his era. Focusing on the issue of voting rights, he used the familiar cadence and antiphony of the Baptist sermon to involve his audience. "Give us the ballot," he proclaimed as he began each statement. Soon their voices echoed his and punctuated his words with a chorus of "amens."

Afterward, New York's *Amsterdam News* wrote that King "emerged from the Prayer Pilgrimage to Washington as the number one leader of sixteen million Negroes in the United States."

Students of history always try to understand what makes great leaders of men. Why was Martin Luther King, Jr., able to galvanize his people so they would follow wherever he led? Why was it he to whom they looked, in whom they believed? What enabled him to go where none had gone before and bring his people with him?

Many of those who were close to him agree with the explanation of Reverend C. T. Vivian, who first met Dr. King at the Prayer Pilgrimage and eventually became the director of affiliates for SCLC. "Martin was saying what I wished I could say, and he was in fact enunciating my deepest understanding of what it was all about."

Rufus Lewis was the man who nominated Dr. King to be the president of the Montgomery Improvement Association. "His greatest personal contribution," Lewis later said, "was interpreting the situation to the mass of the people. He could speak better than any man that I've ever heard in expressing to the people their problem and making them see clearly what the situation was and inspiring them to work at it."

King was the voice through whom every black in Montgomery, and later across the South and throughout the nation, was speaking his own innermost feelings. One member of his congregation was heard to say to him, "Reverend, you have the words that we're thinking but can't say."

"He and I talked about it sometimes," says Jo Ann Robinson. "Somewhere in history, he was destined to be there. He knew what to say and how to say it. He had a tone that could reach each one—

white or black."

But those who knew him also agree that a great deal more than words drew people to Martin Luther King. "Dr. King never lost this touch; he never was out of touch with the common, everyday man," insists Richmond Smiley, a deacon of Dexter Avenue Baptist Church. William Nix, King's counselor at Morehouse and a member of his family's church in Atlanta, adds, "Love, compassion, understanding, leadership, confidence, courage. He became a symbol, and disenfranchised people across the world were looking at this symbol. In this symbol they saw hope."

"He just had courage," according to Rufus Lewis, "and he inspired courage in the rest of the folks who lacked it. He felt the pains of the people. He was just that type of person. I don't think there was any external thing that made him say, 'I'm going to give my life for this,' " Lewis adds. "He just did it."

"He had the method, the means, and he was the man," explains Reverend Vivian. "That method was built upon our faith. Because our faith says you turn the other cheek. This is what people have heard all their lives. When Martin said we couldn't win a violent encounter, we knew he was right.

"The other thing is you could do something by doing nothing. You've got to see the power of that method. People were thinking to themselves, 'I don't have to get on the bus. Nobody can break my leg for not getting on the bus. Nobody can burn me for not getting on the bus.' You can't force somebody to get on the bus. They already knew they had it won, the way Martin was talking. That was the method itself.

"And then he constructed the means, working with people in a way they were all involved. He wasn't the only thing happening.

"The method, the means, and the *man*. Martin *was* what he talked about. People saw in Martin a person who, in fact, loved them. They saw in Martin a person who was nonviolent. You see, his character came through. They knew he was what he said. And you don't fool black people very easily on that."

King's leadership qualities were admired not only by those who would be followers, but also by many such as Vivian, who were already leaders of their own movements. "His depth was the thing that was beyond what we had been accustomed to in the nonviolent activities and actions of which I had formerly been a part," explains Vivian. "Because Martin understood at a whole depth level that we had not dealt with. Ours was more method. His was con-

ception. You could see both the mind of the man and the courage of the man. He was really where he was supposed to be—and you knew that."

For some, he was more than a man. R. D. Nesbitt, was chairman of the pulpit committee that brought Dr. King to Dexter Avenue Baptist Church. "The young people just envisioned a new hope and a new day, and the old folks saw in him a black Jesus. They used to love to call him 'My boy' or 'My son.' They worshipped him."

"This was the most stimulating thing in the lives of most of the Negroes in this area," says Lewis, referring to Montgomery's black population. "They have never had anything to equal this in their whole lifetime. I don't believe that there is anything to equal the inspiration and the hope and the love in this last one hundred years. He lifted them so high, and they just can't help but think he is a messiah. They can't help it, no matter how smart they are."

Many continue to ask themselves—as with all great historical figures—did the man make the times or the times make the man? "I can't really understand it," answers Smiley, "except to say that perhaps it was an act of God. I believe that: that this young man would come into a community, prepared in every way, and be accepted by the established leadership of the community and would be thrust into the limelight with total support from ministers, businessmen, teachers, and especially the ordinary, common working man."

"I will always believe that the Lord had his hands on Dr. King in everything that he did," adds Arthur Henderson, deacon of Ebenezer Baptist Church. "He was guided by the hands of God."

He had just begun to make his mark when *Time* wrote: "Martin Luther King, Jr., is, in fact, what many a Negro—and, were it not for his color, many a white—would like to be." Although King's preeminence aroused some jealousy among the older, more established black leaders, he constantly reiterated the need to join forces and work together. On many occasions in the future of the movement, he would defer to men like NAACP's Roy Wilkins in order to be assured of their support.

Shortly after the Prayer Pilgrimage to Washington, King became the youngest recipient of the NAACP's prestigious Spingarn Medal for his contribution to race relations.

In June, he and Abernathy were invited to meet with Vice-President Nixon, but the chief result of their discussion was a White House conference a year later, attended by King, Randolph, Wilkins, and Lester B. Granger of the National Urban League. Neither meeting seemed to have any perceptible effect on the policies of the Eisenhower administration. King later wrote of the president, "His conservatism was fixed and rigid. Any evil facing the nation had to be extracted bit by bit with a tweezer because the surgeon's knife was an instrument too radical to touch this best of all possible societies."

In the year between the two White House meetings, however,

Senator Lyndon B. Johnson had managed to push a watered-down Civil Rights Act through Congress—the first since Reconstruction. Though only a partial victory for the civil rights movement, the compromise bill did create the Civil Rights Division of the Justice Department.

Before 1957 came to a close, the Kings' second child, Martin Luther III, was born. King was on the road almost full-time now, giving guest sermons across the country and speaking on behalf of the SCLC and the Montgomery Improvement Association. He was not only the chief fund-raiser for these organizations, but also an important resource for such black groups as the NAACP. Between speaking engagements, he devoted himself to his church and to writing *Stride toward Freedom,* his personal account of the Montgomery story.

In spite of his grueling schedule, he found time that September to meet a young black boy from Troy, Alabama, who wanted to go to college near his home. Even though their efforts were ultimately unsuccessful, John Lewis, who would later work closely with King as the head of the Student Nonviolent Coordinating Committee (SNCC), was impressed in that first encounter with King's sensitivity and concern for the individual.

"I had sent a letter to Dr. King," remembers Lewis, "saying to him that I was a student at American Baptist Theological Seminary, and I would be home for the holidays, and I wanted to talk with

him about going to Troy State College—which was all white. And I had applied to go there, had sent an application, and hadn't heard anything from them. So, Dr. King sent me a letter back inviting me to come to Montgomery to meet with him and Reverend Abernathy and the attorney for the Montgomery bus boycott, Fred Gray.

"Attorney Fred Gray picked me up at the bus station and took me to the First Baptist Church in downtown Montgomery, pastored by Reverend Abernathy. In the Pastor's study when I arrived were Martin Luther King, Jr., and Reverend Abernathy. And it was amazing to me, as I look back on it, that this man, Martin Luther King, Jr., didn't know anything about me—just this poor, barefooted boy from rural Pike County—that he would respond and invite me to come up and have a meeting with him.

"He was very, very sensitive. He really wanted to know about my family and why I really wanted to go to Troy State. And he offered all kinds of support and assistance. When it came time to file the suit to go to Troy State University, my mother and father decided against it. They were afraid of the economic retaliations because of my father's farm being there. They had to live there in 1958."

In 1958, the SCLC established its offices in Atlanta, and Ella Baker was appointed the first executive secretary. Its first official project was a voter registration drive, called the Crusade for Citizenship. On Lincoln's birthday, simultaneous mass meetings were held in twenty-one cities throughout the South. The announced goal was to double the number of black voters. The leaders had chosen this issue carefully because "the right to vote does not raise the issue of social mixing to confuse the main argument." King hoped that by focusing on voting rights, they would be able to attract the support of southern white moderates.

In August, the Kings were paid a visit by one of Mahatma Gandhi's chief lieutenants, Ranganath Diwakar. Talking with the author of a fundamental handbook on nonviolent action, *Satyagraha,* Dr. King was inspired to "think more deeply about the whole philosophy of nonviolence" and became increasingly convinced that, like Gandhi, he must set an example of physical suffering.

Less than a month later, the Montgomery police gave him an opportunity to translate these thoughts to action. On September 3, the Kings accompanied Ralph and Juanita Abernathy to court, where Abernathy was to testify against a man who had assaulted him. When the guard refused to admit them to the courtroom, Dr. King asked

Deacon R. D. Nesbitt chaired the Pulpit Committee that brought King to Dexter Avenue Baptist Church.

Deacon Richmond Smiley volunteered to drive King to his many meetings and engagements in Montgomery and felt personally responsible for his safety.

to speak with Fred Gray, the MIA attorney. "Boy," the officer snarled, "if you don't get the hell out of here, you'll need a lawyer!" Before King could reply, he was seized by two guards, who twisted his arm into a hammerlock and led him to the police station.

When Coretta started to follow her husband, one of the guards said, "You want to go too, gal? Just nod your head." Before she could answer, her husband quickly said, "Don't say anything, darling."

King was charged with loitering, but when Commissioner Sellers learned of the blunder on the part of the officers, he was released. Nevertheless, in court two days later, he was found guilty of refusing to obey an officer and fined ten dollars plus court costs. Taking his example from Gandhi, King decided to go to jail rather than pay the fine. "Your Honor," he said, "I could not in good conscience pay a fine for an act that I did not commit and above all for brutal treatment that I did not deserve." But while he waited to be transported to the jail, King was released. Calling King's action a publicity stunt, Commissioner Sellers had paid the fine, saying he had "elected to spare the taxpayers of Montgomery the expense of feeding and housing [King] during the next fourteeen days."

King pledged never again to pay a fine for a charge arising "from our fight for freedom" and proclaimed, "We have a mandate from God to resist evil. . . . We must go out and no longer be afraid to go to jail."

Two weeks later, on a promotion tour for his new book, *Stride toward Freedom,* King sat at an improvised desk in the shoe department of Blumstein's, a white-owned store in Harlem. As he was autographing copies, a black woman pushed her way toward him and asked, "Are you Mr. King?"

"Yes, I am," he nodded.

"Luther King," she cried, "I been after you for five years!" As she spoke, she drew a sharp, bright object from her dress and thrust it into his chest. Then she continued to beat him with her fists, babbling incoherently. Someone quickly grabbed the woman, who was identified as Mrs. Izola Curry. At the Harlem police headquarters, the forty-two-year-old "rootless wanderer" told the police "people are torturing me" and talked wildly about how ministers were responsible for all her troubles.

King was rushed to the hospital, where surgeons were forced to remove one of his ribs and part of his breastbone to free the Japanese letter opener that was leaning against the main artery from his heart. "If you had sneezed during all those hours of waiting, your aorta would have been punctured and you would have drowned in your own blood," said his physician, Dr. Aubre D. Maynard. The doctor made a cross-shaped incision over King's heart. "Since the scar will be there permanently, and he is a minister, it seemed somehow appropriate," he said.

Still under sedation, his first words to his wife were a minister's words: "Coretta, this woman needs help. She is not responsible for the violence. Don't do anything to her; don't prosecute; get her healed."

King received messages of sympathy from all over the world, including telegrams from President Eisenhower and Vice-President Nixon. But one letter in particular he would never forget.

Dear Dr. King,

I am a ninth grade student at the White Plains High School. While it shouldn't matter, I would like to mention that I'm a white girl. I read in the paper of your misfortune and of your suffering. And I read that if you had sneezed you would have died. I'm simply writing you to say that I'm so happy that you didn't sneeze.

Chapter Six

The
Method
of
Nonviolence

*Nonviolent resistance . . . is based on the
conviction that the universe is on the side
of justice. Consequently, the believer
in nonviolence has deep faith in the
future. This faith is another reason
why the nonviolent resister can accept
suffering without retaliation. For
he knows that in his struggle for
justice he has cosmic companionship.*

MLK, Jr.

IN THE WEEKS following his near-fatal stabbing, King found himself, for the first time in many months, with the peace and solitude for contemplation and quiet meditation. He used the opportunity to review his work, his goals, and his philosophy of nonviolence. He was moving toward a formal acceptance of Gandhian nonviolence, and it occurred to him that his current tribulation was only a fraction of the suffering he would have to endure for the cause of freedom. His doctors recommended that he remain out of the heat of battle until he regained his strength. So he decided to accept a long-standing invitation from the Gandhi Peace Foundation to make a month-long speaking tour of India.

Ten years after the assassination of the great leader, King found the spirit of Gandhi very much alive in India, and he judged the Mahatma to be "by all standards of measurement . . . one of the half dozen greatest men in world history." To bring the British domination of his country to an end, Gandhi had been jailed many times, had fasted to near-starvation, had been physically assaulted, and throughout had continued to reject violence as a weapon.

King's trip to India solidified his own commitment to nonviolent direct action, which was becoming the guiding principle of his character and his work. He perceived the philosophy of nonviolent resistance as Christianity in action. Later, he would say that Christ had furnished the spirit and the motivation while Gandhi had provided the method.

For King, the ultimate goal of his own Christian ministry and, by extension, the civil rights movement was to create what he called the "beloved community"—a community based on love where people would be judged "not on the basis of the color of their skin, but on the content of their character." The "beloved community" would reject as unjust any law that debased an individual and robbed him of his dignity.

In defining the "beloved community," King was establishing his own brand of the social gospel that had impressed him so as a student. It focused on improving life in this world. He agreed with the Christian social philosopher Rauschenbusch that "a Christian preacher should have the prophetic insight which discerns and champions the right before others see it."

"I heard him say that he'd rather die than be subjected to something that he knew wasn't right," remembers Mrs. Lavata Lightner, who had known him from childhood.

"Dr. King felt very strongly, as I do, that our civil rights involvement was merely an extension of our Christian ministry," explains Reverend Ralph Abernathy. "He made that very clear, over and over again, just as Jesus did when he went into the temple and read, 'The Spirit of the Lord is upon me, because he hath anointed me to preach the gospel to the poor; he hath sent me to heal the broken-hearted, to preach deliverance to the captives, to set at liberty them that are bruised, and then to proclaim the Kingdom of the Lord.' Any Christian minister must be involved in the human rights struggle. We cannot preach the gospel in the four walls of the church and let it stop there. We must take it into the streets and let Jesus live in the hearts and minds and souls and bodies of all individuals."

King preached that the "beloved community" could be achieved only through love. To explain the form of love that must guide his people in the nonviolent movement, King encouraged his congregation to examine the meanings of the three Greek words for love. *Eros,* he explained, is romantic love; *philia* is the intimate affection between friends; *agape* is goodwill and understanding toward all men. According to King, it is *agape* that enables us to love every man, not because we like him or his customs, but solely because God loves him. When the Old Testament commands us to "Love Thy Neighbor," it refers to this form of love. When Jesus said, "Love your enemies," this was the love of which he spoke. But, wrote King, Jesus did not command us to "like your enemies." *Agape* is the only form of love that is unconditional. It does not distinguish between worthy and unworthy persons.

"He'd like to see people accepted for what they are," explains William Nix, one of those who was moved by Dr. King's sermons at Ebenezer. "He'd like to see people helped for what they might become. He saw some good in everybody." He believed "that the whites and blacks should be brothers; that we are all brothers and should act like brothers," adds Rufus Lewis.

In addition to providing the foundation of love, Christianity went a step further. It said, "Turn the other cheek." In the early days of the Montgomery boycott, these traditional elements of Christianity formed the underpinnings of the nonviolent philosophy. These beliefs were already familiar to King's nonviolent army. He was preaching ideas that were basic to their Christian faith. But, he was transforming ideas to action.

It was the philosophy of Gandhi, merged with traditional Christianity, that would provide King with the means to make that transformation and thereby to arouse the conscience of the nation. "The

Christian doctrine of love," he wrote, "operating through the Gandhian method of nonviolence, is one of the most potent weapons available to an oppressed people in their struggle for freedom."

King found special meaning in Gandhi's concept of "satyagraha," which is literally translated "holding on to truth" and has been called "truth-force." Gandhi devoted himself to the constant pursuit of truth. To him, God and truth were synonymous, so truth-force was also soul-force. Gandhi had proven in India that through suffering without fear or hatred—through soul-force—he could appeal to the conscience and heart of his opponent. "Through our pain," he prophesied, "we will make them see their injustice."

King was coming to agree with Gandhi both that it was wrong to support unjust laws and, beyond that, that it was right to resist such a law, even if it meant going to jail. Both leaders were familiar with St. Augustine's assertion that "an unjust law is no law at all." If unjust laws exist—laws that dehumanize and degrade certain members of a society—how do we change those laws? asked King. Some of his contemporaries believed that the battle against unjust laws should be fought in the courts. But King, like Gandhi and Henry David Thoreau, believed that oppressed people must defy unjust laws. "The law," wrote Thoreau, "will never make men free; it is men who have got to make the law free." King saw the civil rights movement as "an outgrowth of Thoreau's insistence that evil must be resisted and no moral man can patiently adjust to injustice."

Both King and Gandhi had been influenced by Thoreau's essay *On the Duty of Civil Disobedience*. "Must the citizen ever for a moment, or in the least degree resign his conscience to the legislator?" asked Thoreau. "Why has every man a conscience then? I think that we should be men first and subjects afterward. It is not desirable to cultivate a respect for the law so much as for the right. The only obligation which I have a right to assume is to do at any time what I think right."

Gandhi echoed Thoreau's belief, saying that even if you are a minority of one, the Truth is the Truth, and time after time he went willingly to jail to protest an unjust law.

"There comes a time," King frequently said, "when a moral man can't obey a law which his conscience tells him is unjust. And the important thing is that when he does that, he willingly accepts the penalty—because if he refuses to accept the penalty, then he becomes reckless, and he becomes an anarchist. There were those individuals in every age and generation who were willing to say, 'I will be

obedient to a higher law.' It is important to see that there are times
when a man-made law is out of harmony with the moral law of the
universe."

King was entering new territory. The first phase of the movement—Montgomery—had involved a classic passive resistance action.
No laws were broken. Now King recognized that the next phase of
the movement required civil disobedience. King differed somewhat
from Thoreau in the matter of method and from Gandhi in his ultimate purpose. Thoreau did not advocate nonviolence and, in fact,
was an anarchist who was opposed to any form of government.
Gandhi, although an unswerving proponent of nonviolence, sought
ultimately to overthrow British rule in India. Martin Luther King, and
indeed all of those participating in the movement for the next decade,
did not seek to overthrow the existing government or disrupt the
political system. They struggled only to be allowed to participate in
it fully, to enjoy the benefits that were constitutionally promised to
all Americans. "We just want to be free," King pronounced. "We
are not seeking to dominate the nation politically or hamper its social
growth; we just want to be free."

To achieve that freedom, King sought to arouse the conscience
of the nation and the world. "How do you reach the conscience of
a nation, so that it does that thing which is right? You do it in a way
that you are willing to be the sufferer," explains King's colleague
Reverend Vivian. "No one can complain when you're doing it that
way because you're saying, 'We're acting out of love. If we're wrong,
it's only we that will suffer in the end.' "

At the core of King's conviction was the belief that people would
choose good over evil, but the choice must always be undeniably
clear. Good must stand apart—untainted, unblemished. Without
moral superiority, King insisted, blacks would confront whites on a
common battlefield, but with vastly inferior ammunition. King knew
the blacks could never win a violent confrontation. But his commitment to nonviolence went far beyond this pragmatic reasoning. He
condemned violence as immoral. He recognized that nonviolence
called upon something in human nature that made hatred decrease
and respect increase.

The goal of nonviolent protest is to make injustice visible. First,
the oppressed must have a just cause. Then, through their pain,
they force the oppressor to see the injustice. "He was representing
an oppressed minority," explains William Nix of Morehouse College. "He struck the consciousness of a sensitive silent majority. I

think that not all of white America was as bad as it had been painted, but very few people had reached their conscience. So attitudes changed as they saw Negroes being watered down with fire hoses, as they saw innocent people being killed by police brutality, as they saw innocent children being bombed in churches. There was a reaction to this type of thing."

King, like Gandhi, rejected the idea that nonviolence meant meek submission to the will of the oppressor and felt the term "passive resistance" was a misnomer. On the contrary, nonviolent resistance is active and provocative. It requires great courage, for the nonviolent warrior must say to himself, "I will not fight but I will not comply." And in the end, he must go even farther, acknowledging, "I am not willing to kill, but I am willing to die."

King frequently addressed this issue. "If such physical death is the price that we must pay to free our children from a life of permanent psychological death, then nothing could be more honorable."

He believed with Gandhi in the redemptive power of unearned suffering, and he urged his followers to say to their opponents, "We shall match your capacity to inflict suffering by our capacity to endure suffering. We shall meet your physical force with soul-force. Do to us what you will, and we shall continue to love you. We cannot in all good conscience obey your unjust laws, because noncooperation with evil is as much a moral obligation as is cooperation with good. Throw us in jail, and we shall still love you. Send your hooded perpetrators of violence into our community at the midnight hour and beat us and leave us half dead, and we shall still love you. But be ye assured that we will wear you down by our capacity to suffer."

His words were new and difficult to his flock. It was not enough merely to preach them. He would have to teach and train those who would be his followers. Richmond Smiley was one of those in Montgomery. "Now here comes a man," remembers Smiley, "who tells you that you had to face brutal policemen and other people with no protection for yourself, and not only that, but do not strike back. We had never heard of this type of movement. And so Dr. King had to train, if you want to use the word. Most certainly he had to change the thinking of the entire community."

"Our forefathers often bragged," Smiley continues, "that they had never been to jail. You were a good man if you had never been to jail. To say now, 'Go to jail if they arrest you, but go in dignity with your head up.' To many of us it would have been an act of cowardice if somebody had hit you, and you did not hit them back.

Previous page: **King and the SCLC forged a coalition of conscience that brought clergymen of all faiths into the nonviolent civil rights movement.**

Above: **The method of nonviolent resistance requires self-discipline and total commitment.**

"Through our pain," said Gandhi, "we will make them see their injustice."

It meant that you were weak. But he gave us a different feeling, a different meaning of life. In other words, he brought to us that the one suffering the abuse of others was not necessarily the coward. Perhaps the one inflicting the abuse was really the coward.''

Arthur Henderson, senior deacon of Ebenezer Baptist Church, says he questioned the new philosophy in the beginning. "And I wondered how far he could go with it, because I guess I was like the average man realizing how mean and low-down these white people have been over the years and how they mistreated the black man. And yet, I'd stop and look at it and I'd say, 'Now this is the teaching of Jesus.' Because he said: 'If you are struck on the left cheek, turn the right; and if you are struck on the right cheek, turn the left.' And this is what nonviolence was saying, 'Just turn the other side.' I began to see how effective it was because the meanest of the white people didn't know how to fight nonviolence. And when you don't fight back, it is hard to fight."

"Nonviolence was the solution," agrees Rufus Lewis. "If they hit you, don't hit back. I think this is the thing that disarmed the opposition because they didn't know how to cope with nonviolence. It's not a natural reaction if somebody slaps you not to slap them back. You are going to either slap them back or run in fear. If you don't do either of these things, then they don't know exactly how to cope. If you start beating me, and I don't do anything, you can't just keep on hitting me without having some feeling about it. And you stop. I hope you would."

King recognized that nonviolence was not easy and that it required constant encouragement and training. "It is difficult at times to convince people that this is the best way," he told a British television audience. "And I guess it is difficult for all of us not to retaliate. But on the whole, I have been amazed at the tremendous response that we have gained when we have called for nonviolent action. I look back over Montgomery and think of the fact that for all of these days, three hundred and eighty-one days, more than ninety-nine and nine-tenths percent of the Negro citizens participated in the boycott. They confronted harrassing experiences; they confronted physical violence. And never did they retaliate with a single act of physical violence. Even though it is difficult, I think we have been able to get this method over in a most significant way."

During the Montgomery protest and in the subsequent years, King worked closely with other proponents of nonviolence to train blacks in the techniques of nonviolent resistance. Jim Lawson, a Nashville minister and a member of the Fellowship of Reconciliation (FOR), has been called the guru of nonviolence by many who participated in the movement.

Under his expert guidance, FOR produced a pamphlet entitled "How to Practice Nonviolence" that became a bible for demonstrators. "Nonviolence," the brochure explained, "is a way of overcoming injustice, not of retaliating for it. Basically it is rooted in the recognition that your opponent is human. Being human, he will probably react with fear if you threaten him, but in the long run he is likely to respond with good will if you go out of your way to encourage it. Don't expect immediate results. Your opponent's first reaction may be surprise that you have not answered injustice with injustice. He may then become exasperated that you are not 'talking his language,' and he may try to provoke you further, try to incite you to violence.

"He will probably be very suspicious and think that you are planning to trick him in some secret way, or he may think that your nonviolence stems from weakness, and try to take advantage of you. But gradually, if you hold fast to your nonviolent program, your opponent will gain respect for you. If your campaign succeeds, it will not be by defeating him but by removing his hostility."

John Lewis, later the head of SNCC and described by *Time* magazine as "a living saint," was one of those trained by Lawson. "You can accept nonviolence as a technique or as a tactic, or you can accept it as a philosophy, a way of life, a way of living," explains Lewis. "And if you do just accept it as a technique or a tool in a particular situation, you must come to that point where you believe in it so that it cuts across your entire life, your whole life. It becomes personal; it becomes part of you. And you don't say today, 'Well, I'm going to be nonviolent and maybe tomorrow I'll do something else.' "

Reverend Jimerson agrees. "Nonviolence is a commitment. It's a dedication. It isn't just something you say. One has to be dedicated to nonviolence in order to follow it."

Richmond Smiley served as a driver for Dr. King and considered himself a self-appointed bodyguard. In that role, he was ambivalent about nonviolence. "When I was driving Dr. King it turned real cold one night, and, of course, Dr. King kept requesting that I turn the heat on. I was unable to turn this heater on for a good reason, and that was that I had kept unbeknownst to Dr. King a little Italian [revolver] in the slot in which the heat would come from the heater in the car. I felt that this was a very good place to keep it; I did not want to embarrass him or get in trouble myself if we were stopped and searched and the gun was found. I was afraid to turn the heat up too high for fear that with this loaded gun in there my secret might be made known to everybody, including Dr. King.

"Later, I told him about it, and this was real funny to him. He had laughed and teased me and said that I was not committed. He would always keep that before you: 'You are not committed. I've got to talk with you; I've got to do something for you,' he would say."

King's own commitment was unwavering. "When things were perhaps at their worst, he was still able to prevail on this policy of nonviolence and love," according to Nix. "I think it takes a strong man in the face of an enemy to accept all of this without using some type of weapon to fight back. So I think he was a very special type of man who came along when history needed him most."

"I think Martin Luther King, Jr., was in a sense a radical Christian," says John Lewis. "And that the philosophy and the concept of nonviolence is radical—to use good to overcome evil. I think you can be militant, and you can be aggressive, and you can be nonviolent. To be nonviolent is different from being non-aggressive."

King understood this, perhaps better than ever before, when he returned from India, rested and recuperated and ready for his next campaign. "We have a power," he proclaimed, "power that can't be found in Molotov cocktails, but we do have a power. Power that cannot be found in bullets and guns, but we have a power. It is a power as old as the insights of Jesus of Nazareth and as modern as the techniques of Mahatma Gandhi."

The nonviolent method relied on sit-ins, boycotts, marches, and demonstrations.

Chapter Seven

Fill
the
Jails

The nonviolent approach does not immediately
change the heart of the oppressor. It
first does something to the hearts and
souls of those committed to it. It gives
them new self-respect; it calls up resources
of strength and courage that they did not
know they had. Finally it reaches the
opponent and so stirs his conscience
that reconciliation becomes a reality.

MLK, Jr.

UPON HIS RETURN from India, King was ready to take his beliefs a step farther than he had gone in Montgomery. The protestors in Montgomery had not set out to break the law. They simply refrained from riding the bus. They had won by "not doing." Now King was coming to accept the necessity of "doing"—specifically of refusing to obey an unjust law. Philosophically, he had made the leap from passive resistance to civil disobedience.

In late November 1959, he made the "painful decision" to leave the Dexter Avenue Baptist Church in Montgomery and return to Atlanta, where the SCLC had established its headquarters. There he would also join his father as assistant pastor at Ebenezer. "I can't stop now," he told his tearful congregation. "History has thrust something upon me which I cannot turn away. I should free you now." Reluctantly, the church members accepted his resignation, knowing their minister was destined to serve on a grander scale.

In his public announcement of his impending move to Atlanta, King said, "The time has come for a broad, bold advance of the southern campaign for equality. . . . We must train our youth and adult leaders in the techniques of social change through nonviolent resistance. We must employ new methods of struggle, involving the masses of the people."

As if in response to his call, just over a month later, black students in Greensboro, North Carolina, spontaneously took seats at a segregated lunch counter. Their action ignited a student revolt throughout the state, and the sit-in movement began.

Joseph McNeill, a student at the all-black North Carolina Agricultural and Technical College, tried on January 31, 1960, to get something to eat at the Greensboro bus terminal's lunch counter. He was refused with a curt "We don't serve Negroes." McNeill and his roommate, Ezell Blair, Jr., decided to undertake their own nonviolent protest. The next day, two other students joined them as they took seats at the lunch counter. Refused service, they continued this action every day. Within two weeks, students throughout North Carolina were demanding integrated service in department stores and bus terminals.

John Lewis recalls events that helped spread the movement throughout the South. Jim Lawson, the Methodist minister who was training Nashville students, including Lewis, in nonviolence "received a telephone call from an old friend of his—a Methodist minister named Douglas Moore—saying, 'What can the students in Nashville do to be supportive of the students in North Carolina?' And

Jim told him what we were doing and what we were planning. Two or three days later, we had a mass rally in the chemistry building on the Fisk University campus. More than five hundred students showed up. And we went through a quick lesson in the philosophy and the discipline of nonviolence. On the next day, we had to be prepared to go and sit-in. And, to me, it became like a holy crusade. It was one of the most moving, one of the most exciting moments, really, to see these young black college students and a few white college students from some of the other colleges and universities.

"We were dressed like we were going to church or going out on a very special date or something. It was just a different climate. The young ladies had their stockings and their heels; all the guys would put on ties and coats. And you go there and you sit-in all day. They made you start at ten in the morning, and you would sit at that lunch counter all day. And if you had to leave to go to a class, another person would come and take your place. And you'd just sit there, and you'd have your book and just read and study, bring your homework or whatever.

"During that period, Dr. King came in and out of Nashville constantly. He would say that the Nashville student movement was the most organized, the most disciplined. And he would salute the students and pay tribute to Jim Lawson."

By the end of March, the nonviolent sit-ins had spread to more than fifty southern cities. Although he had not initiated the sit-in movement, King was the symbolic leader for many of the students. With Montgomery as their inspiration, they would now interpret the technique of nonviolence in their own way, pushing the movement to a new plateau. Their tactics were sometimes more radical than King would have chosen, but in the crucible of the student movement was forged a new generation of black leaders, many of whom would become his team in the years ahead.

"I remember very well the influence of Martin Luther King, Jr., on the national movement," recollects Lewis. "We had been told in late February that if we would go downtown on a particular day, we would be arrested. The local police officials would allow these young men, the Klan types, to beat us up. There had been an incident where a lighted cigarette had been put out in the head of a young woman. They would come and pour ketchup or mustard over people, grab people off of the lunch counter stool. You had a great deal of that, but no one would get charged.

"So the night before the demonstration, a friend of mine, who was named Bernard Lafayette, who was a student at American Baptist Seminary, the two of us, it was our responsibility to draw up some dos and don'ts for the sit-ins. We wrote things like, 'Don't talk back. Sit up straight. Don't lash out. Don't hit back.' And finally we said something like 'Remember the teachings of Jesus, of Gandhi, and Martin Luther King, Jr. May God bless you.'

"Every single student that went down that day had these little dos and don'ts on them, in their pockets or someplace in a book. When they got arrested, the police officials tried to make a big thing out of it. 'This was a conspiracy,' and all of that because they all had the same thing.

"The point I guess I'm trying to make here, the spirit of Martin Luther King, Jr., was very much a part of that movement. Because we kept saying, throughout the sit-in, this is the way Dr. King would have us do it."

King's most significant impact on the student sit-in movement was his contribution to structuring it. During the first months, the students acted spontaneously with little or no effective organization. But in April, the Student Nonviolent Coordinating Committee (SNCC) was born.

"SNCC was organized Easter weekend, between April 16 and 20, 1960, in Raleigh, North Carolina," remembers Lewis, who would later be its chairman. "SNCC was really founded by the Southern Christian Leadership Conference. Ella Baker, who was executive assistant to Dr. King, was asked by Dr. King to put together a youth leadership conference." The students invited were not the presidents of the student body or the heads of a fraternity or sorority. They were the young people who had emerged in the local civil rights movements.

"Jim Lawson was there almost like a hero," according to Lewis, "because he was this person that the students, particularly from Nashville, really rallied behind. There was a debate over whether the organization should be an arm of SCLC or whether it should be an independent operation. Ella Baker was on the staff at SCLC, but she felt it should be an independent group, and Jim Lawson felt the same. Some people tried to get Jim Lawson to be the head of a new organization, but he wanted to play an advisory role. There was a debate whether the office of the organization should be located in Atlanta or located in Nashville. The Atlanta people won."

At a second meeting in October, SNCC became a permanent organization, and Marion Barry was elected president. Lewis

Previous page: *The nonviolent sit-ins, Freedom Rides, and demonstrations were met with anger and hatred.*

Above: *King and the nonviolent demonstrators were willing to go to jail to protest an unjust law.*

acknowledges that in spite of later disputes between some members of SNCC and SCLC, the students always felt "a tremendous affection and love and belief in Dr. King."

The sit-ins provoked arrests and outbreaks of violence in some southern cities. Like King, the students were willing to "fill the jails" rather than pay fines or bail. But while King was very much a spiritual symbol whose presence was felt in the movement, his own active participation was limited for a time by a personal legal suit. Alabama officials were claiming that King had committed perjury on his 1956 and 1958 income tax returns.

Although he knew they were trumped-up charges, King felt tremendous shame and concern that his people would think he had betrayed them. His friends in New York, Harry Belafonte, Bayard Rustin, and Stanley Levison, who had contributed considerable sums of money during the Montgomery boycott, promised to raise $200,000 for King's defense, as well as for the needs of the SCLC and student protestors.

The state's case collapsed, however, when Lloyd Hale, a state tax agent, admitted he had found "no evidence of fraud in the preparation of King's income tax return." An all-white southern jury acquitted him on May 28.

In June, King met for the first time with Senator John F. Kennedy, who was by then the front-runner for the Democratic presidential nomination. Although he reported that the meeting was "very fruitful and rewarding," King did not feel it appropriate to endorse any candidate. After the presidential conventions, he was convinced that both parties had been "hypocritical on the question of civil rights."

Meanwhile, throughout the summer, the sit-ins continued. At the urging of student protestors, King participated in a lunch counter sit-in against Rich's, Atlanta's foremost department store. The demonstrators were arrested for trespassing and, refusing to pay bond, went to jail. King promised to "stay in jail ten years if necessary."

When an aid of Senator Kennedy called to question the constitutionality of these arrests, the charges were dropped and all of the demonstrators were released except King. Officials from nearby DeKalb County requested that King be transferred to their custody to stand trial for violating probation on a previous traffic violation. He was convicted and sentenced to four months of hard labor in Georgia's public works camps. On hearing this severe sentence, Coretta, who was five months pregnant with the Kings' third child, broke into tears in public for the first time since the movement began.

King was taken first to the DeKalb County Jail and then transferred three hundred miles from Atlanta to the Reidsville State Penitentiary. Senator Kennedy telephoned the distraught Coretta and promised to do all that he could for her husband. Thanks to his intervention, King was released on a two thousand–dollar bond on October 27.

Although he still did not formally endorse Kennedy for president, King and his associates did everything short of it. Daddy King told his congregation he was switching his vote to Kennedy, and Ralph Abernathy urged blacks to "take off your Nixon buttons." Kennedy captured nearly three-quarters of the black vote, and some would later claim it was this support that gave him his narrow victory.

Shortly after the inauguration, on January 30, 1961, the Kings' third child was born and named Dexter Scott after their cherished church in Montgomery.

In March, the Congress of Racial Equality, backed by the SCLC and SNCC, announced a new campaign—"to put the sit-ins on the road." The project was a major test of strength that involved the whole movement, and a challenge to the Kennedy administration, which seemed at this point to be responding with "critical indecisiveness" to black demands for enforcement of the Supreme Court desegregation decisions and a strong civil rights bill.

In early May, six pairs of volunteers, black and white, joined by a CORE observer, boarded two regularly scheduled Greyhound and Trailways interstate buses in Washington, D.C., to travel through Virginia, the Carolinas, Georgia, Alabama, and Mississippi. The plan was to test the public facilities at each stop, sitting in segregated waiting rooms and seeking service at segregated lunch counters.

John Lewis was among those first Freedom Riders. "The night before we were supposed to leave, on May 4, we had a dinner at a Chinese restaurant, the group of us," recalls Lewis. "When I look back on it, I think that night we sort of joked, saying that this was like the Last Supper. And it really was, in a sense, after you look down the road; it was something like the Last Supper for some of us.

"The freedom ride was to test a Supreme Court decision. The Supreme Court had ruled outlawing segregation in the areas of public transportation, on everything. All across the South, you still saw the signs saying 'White' and 'Colored.' Black people had to buy their tickets out of little holes, little windows, and then go out around to stand or sit down in the so-called colored waiting room. They couldn't eat in the so-called white restaurants, and there were public toilets saying 'Colored Men,' 'Colored Women,' 'White Men,' 'White Women.' You still had to go to the back of the bus if you wanted to travel through the South. The CORE Freedom Ride was what was needed to put an end to segregation in the area of public transportation."

King was in Washington to encourage the first group of riders as they departed. The buses traveled through Virginia without incident, but in North and South Carolina Freedom Riders were arrested. In one case the charges were dropped, and in the other the rider was acquitted by the local judge on the basis of the December Supreme Court decision.

"We left, and went on to Rockhill, South Carolina," Lewis remembers. "When we arrived at Rockhill, Albert Bigelow and myself entered a so-called 'white' waiting room. And the moment we opened the door and started in, a group of young men attacked us, beat us, knocked us down, and the police officials just stood there."

In Alabama, the reception was even uglier. When the Greyhound bus arrived in Anniston, it was greeted by an angry white mob. Armed with iron bars, they smashed windows, punctured tires, and hurled a bomb that set the bus on fire. Some of the Freedom Riders were attacked and beaten as they emerged from the burning bus. Although nine white men were later arrested for their part in the violence, none was ever punished.

The Trailways bus reached Birmingham, where the police stood by while local whites savagely assaulted the Freedom Riders. Throughout these brutal beatings, the protestors adhered to their principles of nonviolence.

CORE, in the meantime, had decided to halt the rides because of the violence. "Bobby Kennedy asked for a 'cooling off' period," says Lewis. "We argued that we wanted to go; the ride had to continue. We couldn't have a 'cooling off' period. We must not show the segregationists that they can stop us by using violent forces. We were able to convince the Nashville Christian Leadership Council, which was the local chapter of the SCLC, to give us the necessary money to buy tickets for ten people to go from Nashville to Birmingham, Birmingham to Montgomery, Montgomery to Jackson, Jackson to New Orleans."

Outside of Birmingham, the bus carrying the riders from Nashville was stopped and boarded by the man who was to become Martin

King and SNCC field secretary Bernard Lafayette, Jr., led one of many nonviolent training sessions for the Freedom Riders.

Luther King, Jr.,'s most publicized adversary—the Birmingham commissioner of public safety, Bull Connor.

"Bull Connor came on the bus with another police official," Lewis recalls. "There was a young guy named Paul Brooks, black, and a young white guy named Jim Swerg. They were sitting on the front seat, right behind the driver. They were asked to move by Bull Connor, and they refused. They were arrested and taken off the bus, taken to jail.

"In the meantime, Bull Connor told other police officials to come. At the bus station, they wanted to know who were the Freedom Riders, but we did not identify ourselves. We just sat there. So they asked to see the tickets. And he literally took over the bus. We showed our tickets, and he saw the stops that people were making. They allowed all the other people to get off, then they put newspaper over the windshield, the back of the bus, over the windows, keeping the members of the media—the press—from seeing what was going on. About one o'clock in the afternoon, he asked us all off, and said he was taking us into protective custody. And they took us to jail. It was on a Wednesday afternoon.

"Early Friday morning, Bull Connor and several police officials and members of the Birmingham media came up to our jail cell and said they were taking us back to Nashville. We refused to cooperate. So they literally picked us up and took us out, put us in these cars— limousines, big cars—and more than a hundred miles from Birmingham, and maybe one hundred thirty-five or one hundred forty miles from Nashville—about half way in between—in someplace called Ardmore, Alabama, literally dropped us off on the highway. At like four o'clock or five o'clock in the morning. And said, 'You can make it back. A bus will be coming along here; you can take a train.' We were really panicked; we were frightened; we didn't know what to do.

"None of us had ever been to this part of Alabama before, didn't know anything about it. But it was north Alabama. And we knew it was Klan territory."

The frightened Freedom Riders eventually found a ramshackle cabin, where an elderly black couple hid them, fed them, and protected them until a driver from Nashville came to pick them up and take them back to Birmingham to continue their journey.

In Birmingham, bus officials were unable to find a driver willing to take the Freedom Riders to Montgomery. "I have only one life to give," one driver was heard to say, "and I'm not going to give it to CORE or the NAACP." The Freedom Riders were held incommunicado in a waiting room of the bus terminal.

"Bobby Kennedy was trying to get the Greyhound officials to find somebody to drive the bus," Lewis explains. "He kept asking, 'Can't you find some colored bus driver?' He said, 'These people have a right to move. They should be able to move out of Birmingham.' Apparently, the attorney general didn't know that they didn't have any black bus drivers, at least in the South, and not in Birmingham, Alabama."

Finally a driver was recruited, and the Freedom Riders had the bus to themselves as they headed to Montgomery. "The agreement was that there would be two officials from Greyhound sitting on the right side of the bus when you first get on. There would be a plane flying over the bus, and every fifteen miles there would be a state patrol car for the ninety-mile trip from Birmingham to Montgomery," explains Lewis.

The first Freedom bus, in
Anniston, Alabama, on May 15,
1961, after angry whites
hurled incendiary bombs.

James Zwerg, a student from the
University of Wisconsin, was viciously
beaten when his Greyhound bus arrived
in Montgomery on May 20.

"Anyway, we got out. We arrived in Montgomery. It was so quiet, so peaceful. We didn't see anything, didn't see anybody. When the bus pulled up, we didn't see a patrol car, didn't see a police car; we didn't see a sign of the plane; we didn't see anything. The moment that we started standing out on the bus step, we saw people coming from all over the place. It was a big mob that grew to several hundred—men, women, children, with baseball bats, iron pipes, chains, everything."

The police were conspicuously absent, leaving the Freedom Riders vulnerable to savage attacks. "Jim Swerg and a young guy by the name of William Barbee and myself were attacked," continues Lewis. "We were literally just beaten. Jim Swerg was caught, and he was white. He stood out, and they saw him as a betrayer, as a 'nigger lover.' He was beaten with chains, a baseball bat. I was hit in the head with a soda crate and was knocked unconscious. Blood was pouring out of my head, and I saw Jim Swerg lying there. Blood was all over him."

The mob action had been anticipated and even condoned several days before when Alabama governor John Patterson declared, "The people of Alabama are so enraged that I cannot guarantee protection for this bunch of rabble rousers."

The attack persisted for twenty minutes before the police appeared, and only when the numbers approached a thousand did police clear the area with tear gas. When a newsman asked Police Commissioner L. B. Sullivan to send for an ambulance, the officer replied, "Every white ambulance in town reports their vehicles have broken down." The violence continued throughout the day until Attorney General Kennedy sent nearly seven hundred U.S. marshals. Even then Governor Patterson insisted the marshals were unnecessary and threatened to arrest them.

Martin King and Ralph Abernathy were on a speaking assignment in Chicago when they heard the news. They rushed back to Montgomery, where Abernathy was still the pastor of the First Baptist Church. "Dr. King couldn't believe what had happened," says Lewis. "He made his statement, abhorring the violence and saying these were brave young people and if they want to continue to ride, the ride was continuing. He was very concerned about the well-being, the physical well-being, of the young people. He suggested that we have a mass meeting that Sunday to solidify the Montgomery community in support of the freedom rides.

"Sunday afternoon, all of us were told to be at the church early,

so we could get in and get a seat. The meeting was not even supposed to convene until about seven o'clock. At around four o'clock
or four-thirty, the church was full, *completely*. Just packed. All of
the Freedom Riders were disguised as members of the choir because
John Doar [Assistant U.S. Attorney General] didn't want us to be
interviewed and didn't want us to talk to the state officials of Alabama until we had been interviewed by officials from the Department of Justice and the FBI. So we were all put in the choir stand.
I had a red cross type patch on my head, so they got a little cap for
me to put on my head. And we sat down from three o'clock until
the meeting started.

"Long before seven, a mob came near the church. They started
throwing stink bombs, and later started burning cars in front of the
church." More than twelve hundred blacks fervently sang "We Shall
Overcome" while the segregationists barraged the church with bottles and stones and fought the U.S. marshals in the streets.

"Dr. King arrived at the church, and that's when he made his call
to President Kennedy," says Lewis. "He came and he spoke to the
crowd and encouraged the crowd to be calm, to be peaceful, that
he had just talked to the President of the United States, and the
president was prepared to act."

But King's anger was barely concealed as he exclaimed: "The
ultimate responsibility for the hideous action in Alabama last week
must be placed at the doorstep of the governor of the state. We
hear the familiar cry that morals cannot be legislated. This may be
true, but behavior can be regulated. The law may not be able to
make a man love me, but it can keep him from lynching me."

Finally, Governor Patterson declared martial law and sent National
Guardsmen to the church. He then called Attorney General Robert
Kennedy to inform him of the deployment. He also told the attorney general that Major General Henry Graham, the guard com-
mander, could not guarantee the safety of Martin Luther King, Jr.
Kennedy was furious. "Have the General call me," he snapped. "I
want him to say it to me. I want to hear a general of the U.S. Army
say he can't protect Martin Luther King, Jr." Patterson backed down.
The church was sealed off, and King and the other blacks were
escorted to safety.

In the next few days, King agreed to serve as the chairman and
spokesperson for the Freedom Rider Coordinating Committee, which
held nonviolent training sessions for the participants. At the last of
these sessions, he told the riders that they "must develop the quiet

Left: *John Lewis, former president of SNCC, remembers being arrested during the Freedom Rides by Birmingham police commissioner Bull Connor and dropped in the middle of "Klan territory."*

Above: *King and Dr. W. G. Anderson were prohibited from leading a demonstration in Albany, Georgia, by Police Chief Laurie Pritchett.*

courage of dying for a cause. We would not like to see anyone die. We all love life and there are no martyrs here—but we are well aware that we may have some casualties."

The following day, twelve Freedom Riders, accompanied by seventeen reporters and six armed soldiers, left for Jackson, Mississippi. "Going to Mississippi in 1961 was a whole different world," says C. T. Vivian. "You knew you could easily be killed there. That was a different level than being on the line where they threw bricks and stuff at you." The contingent made it to Jackson, where they were arrested, and heeding King's call to "fill the jails," they chose to spend two months in jail rather than pay the two hundred–dollar fine.

The rides continued throughout the summer. The list of those who went to jail included Stokely Carmichael, later a chairman of SNCC; Reverend Ralph Abernathy; Wyatt Tee Walker, executive director of the SCLC; King's brother, Reverend A. D. King; Yale chaplain William Sloan Coffin; Reverend James Lawson of FOR; and James Farmer, founder of CORE. Although some of the young people attacked King for not riding with them, most continued to see him as their symbolic leader.

John Lewis feels that King was extremely responsive to the young people in the movement, although he was never able to give his unreserved support to the more radical approach that saw nonviolence as a tactic, not a way of life. "He said over and over again that these young people were offering new leadership," says Lewis. "It was one of the most encouraging things for him to see people sort of take hold of his message and his methods. I think he was greatly pleased with the young people. He listened to people, and he accepted and considered their ideas and their thoughts.

"I think a great majority of the young people in SNCC, the great majority of young people, saw Dr. King as a symbol, as a leader. Personally, I saw him as a hero. I believed in the man. He was like a teacher. He was a source of inspiration."

In November, the Interstate Commerce Commission banned segregation in buses, trains, and supportive facilities. King interpreted the Freedom Rides as "the psychological turning point in our legal struggle."

Although he had been the symbolic leader of the Freedom Rides, King had not originally organized the movement. By the beginning of 1962, he felt the need to spearhead his first major campaign since Montgomery.

The Freedom Rides had injected his SCLC with a new vitality. By this time, Wyatt Tee Walker, a young Baptist minister and veteran of the sit-ins and Freedom Rides, had been appointed permanent executive director. Ralph Abernathy, King's most trusted friend and advisor, had recently moved to Atlanta to assume the pastorship of West Hunter Baptist Church. In addition to the strong leadership of SCLC's founding members, the organization was now attracting a cadre of young rebels who included in their ranks James Bevel, Dorothy Cotton, C. T. Vivian, Dianne Nash, Hosea Williams, Bernard Lafayette, Walter Fauntroy, and Andrew Young, who would later become SCLC's executive director.

The racial situation in Albany, Georgia, seemed to provide an opportunity for action. Local black leaders and SNCC had already established the embryo of a movement in Albany, modeled after the Montgomery Improvement Association. The Albany movement grew out of a Freedom Ride in December 1961, when 10 riders were jailed. In protest, the black community mobilized a march. In all, 560 black marchers were arrested and 300 chose to stay in jail. On the invitation of William G. Anderson and other local leaders, King and his associates arrived in Albany without a precise strategy or clear-cut goals.

With the words, "Get on your walkin' shoes; walk together, children, and don'tcha get weary," King organized the Freedom Movement's first mass confrontation. He stated, "We will wear them down by our capacity to suffer."

Following mass meetings and nonviolence workshops, the blacks of Albany initiated a series of marches on City Hall, sit-ins at libraries and recreational facilities, and prayer vigils. They also embarked on selective buying campaigns in an effort to force merchants to hire black sales clerks, open lunch counters, and use their influence to pressure city hall.

As in Montgomery, a boycott was launched against the city's bus line. Although the bus company agreed to desegragate and hire at least one black driver, protestors decided to wait for a written promise from the city commissioners before they resumed riding buses. No such promise was forthcoming, and the bus company went out of business. Unfortunately, however, the black population of Albany was not large enough to exert effective economic pressure overall.

Albany police chief Laurie Pritchett arrested demonstrators for loitering, parading without a permit, and disturbing the peace. But no clubs, hoses, or dogs were used in Albany.

King's opponents used every possible tactic to discredit the civil rights leader.

Pritchett had done his homework and had decided to deflate the impact of the demonstrations by confronting nonviolence with nonviolence. The arrests were peaceful. Pritchett and his men were polite. In fact, they provided around-the-clock protection for King.

"He about stopped our movement," says U.S. representative Walter Fauntroy of Pritchett, "because he was just so kind. 'You know it's against the law to lie down in the street, Mr. or Madam,' he'd say. 'You know, I'm a law enforcment officer, and if you persist, I'll have to remove you.' 'We'll be very kind, but just get right in the paddy wagon, and we'll take you straight in, and everything will be all right.' 'We understand what you're doing, but I have a job to do, so let's be cooperative. . . .' I knew we were going to have serious trouble with Pritchett."

At no time did the federal government intervene in Albany, even to enforce the constitutional rights of the protestors. Senator Joseph Clark of Pennsylvania complained that there were "areas of our country in which the Constitution is not in effect."

"Martin King thought that we didn't support him in Albany, so that's where he got sort of irritated with me," says Burke Marshall, now John Thomas Smith Professor of Law at Yale University, who was head of the Justice Department's civil rights division. "The trouble is that the District Judge there was just terrible. So it wasn't like Montgomery, where you had Frank Johnson, or even Birmingham, where you had judges who were sort of sane. Down in that part of Georgia, you had a judge who's been on the bench a long time who was impossible. So we didn't have the judicial climate. And, then, we didn't have any single issue.

"President Kennedy was a little irritated with me at one point," Marshall adds. "He said, 'Why can't you do something?' But the problem was what to do other than what I did, which was to call the mayor all the time."

Afterward, King criticized the FBI for cooperating with the Albany police. His comments so incensed J. Edgar Hoover that the powerful FBI director became determined to discredit King. Hoover's allegations that King and the civil rights movement were influenced by communists would be the basis of years of investigations. King was aware of radicals among his followers, and he knew at least one had been a member of the Communist Party. But, personally, he sharply criticized communism, which on its most basic level was antithetical to his deep Christian convictions.

King was arrested on three separate occasions in Albany and chose to serve the sentences. The first time, he was released from jail and told that "an unidentified, well-dressed Negro man" had paid his fine. King later suspected that Pritchett had learned a lesson from Commissioner Sellers in Montgomery and sent someone to pay the fine himself.

On another occasion, King remained in jail for two weeks. From his cell he wrote: "Albany has become a symbol of segregation's last stand almost by chance." Coretta took her two older children to see their father in jail. Only Yoki, who was nearly seven, was old enough to understand and be upset. Her mother tried to explain, "Daddy's gone [to jail] to help people."

In August, after many defeats and no tangible successes in Albany, King called for a Prayer Pilgrimage. More than eighty rabbis, ministers, and laymen arrived in Albany and gathered at City Hall. Police Chief Pritchett ordered the crowd to disperse. When they refused, he arrested them and took them peaceably to jail. In jail, the twenty demonstrators who were white fasted for thirty-six hours, but even their protest had no visible impact on Albany's white population.

King had to count Albany as a failure because he did not succeed in opening up public facilities. The city was as segregated when he left as when he arrived. But later he was able to point to significant effects, if not victories, in Albany. An entire community was mobilized; parks, libraries, and bus lines were closed even to whites; and a new form of protest was introduced—the mass demonstration.

King and his colleagues analyzed what went wrong in Albany. They pointed to the absence of an organized plan; factionalism among the leaders; the lack of a single target; and the low-keyed tactics of Police Chief Laurie Pritchett. "There wasn't any real strategy," says Atlanta's mayor Andrew Young. King himself said, "Our protest was so vague that we got nothing." "Martin King wasn't really in control in Albany," adds Burke Marshall. "It wasn't like it would be in Birmingham."

If nothing else, however, King felt the response of blacks in Albany was a mandate for a better organized, better focused campaign elsewhere. "Albany in fact has proved how extraordinary was the Negro response to the appeal of nonviolence," King said afterward. "Approximately five percent of the total Negro population went willingly to jail. Were that percentage duplicated in New York City, some fifty thousand Negroes would overflow its prisons. If a people can produce from its ranks five percent who will go voluntarily to jail for a just cause, surely nothing can thwart its ultimate triumph."

Martin Luther King, Jr., Birmingham, Alabama, jail.

Chapter Eight

Confrontation in Birmingham

*When, for decades, you have been able to
make a man compromise his manhood
by threatening him with a cruel and unjust
punishment, and when suddenly he turns
upon you and says: "Punish me. I do not deserve
it. But because I do not deserve it, I will
accept it so that the world will know that
I am right and you are wrong," you hardly
know what to do. You feel defeated and
secretly ashamed. You know that this man
is as good a man as you are; that from some
mysterious source he has found the
courage and the conviction to meet
physical force with soul-force.*

MLK, Jr.

"FREE BY 1963" became the black man's battlecry during the one hundredth anniversary year of the Emancipation Proclamation. Birmingham, Alabama, became the battlefield.

Blacks across the country felt betrayed and disillusioned as the occasion for celebration approached. The hope kindled eight years before when the Supreme Court ordered schools desegrated had given way to despair as "all deliberate speed" proved to be very deliberate delay. Even the vice-president of the United States, Lyndon Johnson, was moved to say, "Emancipation was a Proclamation but not a fact."

In Alabama, the NAACP had been outlawed in 1956. "Now that did more to stir me up than anything," says Reverend Fred L. Shuttlesworth, the minister who then proceeded to organize the Alabama Christian Movement for Human Rights to fight for freedom in Birmingham. "My first thought," remembers Shuttlesworth, "was 'they can outlaw an organization, but they cannot outlaw a movement in the hearts of American people who are determined to be free.' "

His city—Birmingham—had been called the most thoroughly segregated city in the South. Martin King had once said to him half-jokingly, "Birmingham is so segregated, we're within a cab ride of being in Johannesburg, South Africa." Birmingham's racist position had long been personified by Theophilus Eugene ("Bull") Connor, the city's commissioner of public safety. "I lived in Birmingham and faced Bull Connor and the raw tyranny of an unchecked and unbridled police department," says Reverend Shuttlesworth. "Many were Klansmen. They had an unwritten rule that if the Klan doesn't stop you, the police will. In Birmingham, Bull Connor said, 'Damn the law. Down here I'm the law.' "

King called Shuttlesworth "one of the nation's most courageous freedom fighters." The Baptist minister was leading the campaign to desegregate buses in Birmingham when a dynamite blast blew the roof off his house. Miraculously, he walked out of the debris without a scratch. As he did, a policeman approached him and whispered, "Reverend, I respect you. I know these people. I didn't think they'd go this far. If I were you, I'd get out of town as quick as I could."

"Officer, you aren't me," Shuttlesworth answered. "And I'm here for the duration. Go back and tell your Klan brothers that if God could save me through this, they'll have to come up with something better. So the fight's on!"

"Birmingham was not a nonviolent city," stresses Atlanta mayor Andrew Young, who was SCLC's project director. "Birmingham was probably the most violent city in America, and every black family had an arsenal. To talk in terms of nonviolence in Birmingham— folks would look at you like you were crazy because they had been bombing black homes. They had been beating up black people, and the blacks thought there was no alternative for them but to kill or be killed."

In the years following the bombing of his home and church, Shuttlesworth continued his courageous fight against the racist power structure of Birmingham, winning legal victories to desegregate parks and swimming pools. But rather than integrate, the city closed down the parks and pools—even to whites.

Although Bull Connor had assured the citizens of Birmingham that there would be no sit-ins in their city, Shuttlesworth led blacks to the lunch counters of all the major department stores. Connor kept his promise to arrest them all within five minutes, but Shuttlesworth was quietly building a cohesive organization of nonviolent protestors. "My philosophy was that we ought to fight for all of it now. Fight for it now," Shuttlesworth says. "That's why in Birmingham the groundwork was laid for future progress and for Dr. King and the SCLC to come in."

In the late summer of 1962, King and his associates decided to accept Shuttlesworth's invitation and "make our stand in Birmingham." King, Shuttlesworth, and Wyatt Walker, executive director of SCLC, drew up the battle plan and designated it Project "C." "C" stood for *confrontation*.

"If Birmingham could be cracked," King later said, "the direction of the entire nonviolent movement in the South could take a significant turn. It was our faith that 'as Birmingham goes, so goes the South.' "

Project "C" was originally scheduled to begin that fall. But the city fathers desperately wanted to keep King and his organization out of Birmingham. In a meeting with the white business leaders, Shuttlesworth stood firm. Unless blacks saw some specific improvements, King and the SCLC were coming. "The movement is moving," he told them, "and we won't stop moving unless we can have some reason. So what can you all offer today? Your only answer is keeping Dr. King out of here. What can you give?" When no concessions were forthcoming, Shuttlesworth left the meeting. "I'm not here to waste time," he said. "I'm out trying to get freedom. So you all meet us when you can talk to us." The group reconvened the following day, and one of the store owners offered to desegregate the water fountains in his store. "Well, we're going to pass on that. We must have toilets," said Shuttlesworth. "Our women can't refresh themselves, and our men need their dignity, so unless the toilets are desegregated, we don't have anything."

The white businessmen balked, and the negotiations came to a standstill. "You don't have to argue with me," Shuttlesworth said. "The fight is on. You asked us to come see if you could keep King out. We want him in. And if I say he comes, he comes in. You can't keep him out by law."

Shuttlesworth then turned to one of the most influential department store owners, saying, "And when we're arrested, we're not going to walk out with the police; they're going to have to drag us out. And if we go to jail, we're going to stay in jail and fast, so that all the press from all over the world will focus on your place. And we won't change, we won't eat, nothing. And that's for your store."

Finally, the white business leaders informally agreed to take down the "white" and "colored" signs on rest room doors. Project "C" was postponed. However, the store owners soon caved in to pressure from Bull Connor and other hardline segregationists, and the signs went back up. Plans for the demonstrations moved forward once again.

Until this time, Birmingham had been governed by Connor and two other commissioners. However, in the spring of 1963, the city was changing over to government by a mayor and city council. Bull Connor was the leading mayoral candidate. Although both of his opponents were admitted segregationists, they were more moderate than he. Fearing that a direct action by blacks would antagonize the white population enough to help Connor win the election, King decided to postpone the demonstrations a second time until after the election. He needed a victory in Birmingham, and he would bide his time.

When the *Birmingham News* appeared on the stands on Wednesday, April 3, 1963, celebrating Albert Boutwell's mayoral victory over Bull Connor, the front-page headline blared: "New Day Dawns for Birmingham."

But even after his defeat, Connor remained King's principal antagonist in Birmingham. In spite of the results of the election,

King, with Reverend Fred L. Shuttlesworth,
during demonstrations to integrate
Birmingham's commercial district.

Connor and the two other city commissioners maintained that they could not legally be removed from office until 1965, when their terms expired. For the duration of the Birmingham movement, the city operated under two governments.

King opened the Birmingham campaign the day after the election, promising to lead demonstrations until "Pharaoh lets God's people go." The activities for the first few days were limited to sit-ins. The Albany protest had taught King the importance of starting cautiously, devising a long-term strategy, and consolidating forces. He spent the early days attempting to rally the support of Birmingham's black community and its leaders. He was surprised to find that many blacks echoed the opinion of Attorney General Robert Kennedy that the protest was ill-timed. Give the new mayor a chance, they said. Without Bull Connor, the situation is certain to improve.

But King had already delayed Project "C" twice, and he agreed with Fred Shuttlesworth that Boutwell was "just a dignified Bull Connor." Shuttlesworth felt they had waited long enough. "There's no difference, as far as I'm concerned, between Boutwell and Bull Connor," he said. "Bull is a roaring bull and Boutwell is a crying bull. So it wouldn't make any difference which one got elected."

King and his co-workers established four goals for the Birmingham protest: the desegregation of lunch counters, fitting rooms, rest rooms, and drinking fountains in department stores; the upgrading and hiring of blacks throughout the industrial and commercial community; amnesty for the demonstrators; and the creation of a biracial committee to work out a timetable for desegregation elsewhere in the city.

Demonstrators were required to participate in extensive training sessions, where they prepared for the physical abuse they might have to endure. Each volunteer was required to sign a commitment card that read: "I hereby pledge myself—my person and body—to the nonviolent movement." The card went on to detail ten commandments of nonviolent behavior:

1. Meditate daily on the teachings and life of Jesus.
2. Remember always that the nonviolent movement in Birmingham seeks justice and reconciliation—not victory.
3. Walk and talk in the manner of love, for God is love.
4. Pray daily to be used by God in order that all men might be free.
5. Sacrifice personal wishes in order that all men might be free.

6. Observe with both friend and foe the ordinary rules of courtesy.
7. Seek to perform regular service for others and for the world.
8. Refrain from the violence of fist, tongue or heart.
9. Strive to be good in spiritual and bodily health.
10. Follow the directions of the movement and of the captain on a demonstration.

The volunteers "were trained to understand that Bull Connor wanted them to fight back," explains Mayor Young, who along with Reverend James Bevel from the Nashville movement, Reverend Bernard Lee, and Dorothy Cotton, director of the SCLC Citizenship Education Program helped recruit and train demonstrators.

On April 6, a group of carefully selected demonstrators marched on City Hall. At a mass meeting the night before, King inspired the protestors with his familiar eloquence: "If I were to seek to give you a blueprint for freedom in Birmingham tonight, I would say first that at this moment we must decide that we will no longer spend our money in businesses that discriminate against Negroes.

"And I know when I say don't be afraid, you know what I mean. Don't even be afraid to die. I submit to you tonight that no man is free if he fears death. But the minute you conquer the fear of death, at that moment you are free. You must say somehow, I don't have much money; I don't have much education; I may not be able to read and write; but I have the capacity to die."

As the marchers approached the government center, the police ordered them to disperse. When they refused, the protestors were quietly escorted to paddy wagons. Connor, too, had learned a lesson from Albany. He remembered Laurie Pritchett's success in combating nonviolence with nonviolence.

Each day the demonstrations grew stronger. So, too, did the Easter boycott of the downtown stores. King had purposely chosen the busy Easter shopping season for the boycott, and, in contrast to their fellows in Albany, Birmingham's black population wielded enough economic clout to make their nonsupport felt.

Meanwhile, Connor decided to move from the streets into the courts. When he secured a court injunction ordering the demonstrators to halt, he believed he had effectively stopped the movement. King had never before violated a court order. However, at a meeting at Harry Belafonte's apartment in New York a month earlier, the civil rights leader and his staff had already decided their course

White racist groups were overtly active in Birmingham, called "the most racist city in America."

of action in the event of such an order. He announced, "This is raw tyranny under the guise of maintaining law and order. We cannot in all good conscience obey such an injunction, which is an unjust, undemocratic and unconstitutional misuse of the legal process."

King told his people, in the words of St. Augustine, that "an unjust law is no law at all." Men, he said, were required only to obey just laws. And he defined a just law as one that "squares with the moral law, or the law of God." As he was to write from his jail cell several days later: ["Any law that uplifts human personality is just. Any law that degrades human personality is unjust. All segregation statutes are unjust because segregation distorts the soul and damages the personality."]

Says Burke Marshall, "I believe that for the most part what Martin King did, and the Southern Christian Leadership did, was protected and justified in the spirit of the Constitution—in the spirit of the law as well as in the spirit of justice."

And so, for the first time, civil disobedience and the nonviolent movement merged. Bull Connor declared, "You can rest assured that I will fill the jail if they violate the laws as long as I am in City Hall."

King announced that he and Abernathy would go to jail on Good Friday, even though he was desperately concerned that there might be no money with which to post bond. "It's better to go to jail with dignity than to accept segregation in humility," he said. Knowing he was more valuable out of jail than in, his aides begged him not to go. As he had so many times before, King decided to let God show him the way. He withdrew to another room to meditate and pray. When he returned a few minutes later, he said, "I don't know what will happen. I don't know where the money will come from. But I have to make a faith act."

On April 12, almost a thousand blacks lined the streets and sang "We Shall Overcome" as King and Abernathy led fifty-three demonstrators toward downtown Birmingham. They had marched only eight blocks when Connor ordered his men to arrest them. King was placed in solitary confinement and was not allowed to make any telephone calls—even to his wife or attorney—for more than twenty-four hours.

That same day, eight Alabama clergymen drafted a public statement to Martin Luther King, Jr., in which they called the demonstrations "unwise and untimely" and urged local blacks to "withdraw support" from the protests. "When rights are consistently denied," they wrote, "a cause should be pressed in the courts and in negotiations among local leaders, and not in the streets."

In response, King wrote his famous "Letter from Birmingham Jail," explaining the philosophy of nonviolence and presenting one of the most cogent justifications for direct action and civil disobedience. Scribing his comments on the margin of a newspaper, King wrote, "I am in Birmingham because injustice is here. . . . Injustice anywhere is a threat to justice everywhere." In answer to the ministers' suggestion that change should happen in the courts, not in the streets, King wrote, "You may well ask, 'Why direct action? Why sit-ins, marches and so forth? Isn't negotiation a better path?' You are quite right in calling for negotiation. Indeed, this is the very purpose of direct action. Nonviolent direct action seeks to create such a crisis and foster such a tension that a community which has constantly refused to negotiate is forced to confront the issue. It seeks so to dramatize the issue that it can no longer be ignored."

To their assertion that the Birmingham demonstrations were badly timed, King replied, "We know through painful experience that freedom is never voluntarily given by the oppressor; it must be demanded by the oppressed. Frankly, I have yet to engage in a direct-action campaign that was 'well-timed' in the view of those who have not suffered unduly from the disease of segregation. For years now I have heard the word 'Wait!' It rings in the ear of every Negro with piercing familiarity. This 'Wait' has almost always meant 'Never.' We must come to see, with one of our distinguished jurists, that 'justice too long delayed is justice denied.' "

In the opinion of Andrew Young, the "Letter from Birmingham Jail" was the turning point in the movement. "That was what really articulated what the problem was all about," says Young. "You learn how important it is to have a well-stated, well-articulated statement that people can rally around; that it is not enough just to complain about injustice here and there. You've got to define it—one, two, three. State your moral case and offer your solutions."

On Monday, a distraught Coretta, who only two weeks before had given birth to the Kings' fourth child, Bernice Albertine, tried to call President Kennedy. Minutes later, his brother, Attorney General Robert Kennedy, returned her call and promised to do everything he could for her imprisoned husband. A few hours later, the president himself telephoned Mrs. King and assured her that he would look into the matter personally. Almost immediately, King was allowed to call home. Only then did he learn of President Kennedy's intervention.

On Easter Sunday, while King remained in jail, several small groups of blacks sought admittance to six white churches. A few, including King's lieutenant Andrew Young, were welcomed cordially by white clergymen. Others were turned away rudely.

King was released from jail when his friend Harry Belafonte raised another fifty thousand dollars to use toward bail. Once again, the singer promised to find whatever money King needed to ensure the eventual release of the demonstrators.

"I think it was out of need," remembers Shuttlesworth, "that we came to a discussion that the children had to be used if we were going to fill the jails." Now the Birmingham movement became a children's crusade. "Children would always come to the meetings with their parents at night," says Shuttlesworth, "and we would talk about how everybody ought to be free."

King was criticized sharply for risking the lives of children in the protests. But that move heightened the impact and hastened the progress of the entire civil rights movement. Later, King would tell the story of the little girl in Birmingham—not more than eight years old—who walked beside her mother in a demonstration. An amused policeman asked her, "What do you want?" She looked into his eyes and answered, "Fee'dom." Although she could barely pronounce it, her meaning was unmistakeable.

Under the leadership of Reverend James Bevel, Birmingham's black students were proselytized and trained in nonviolence. "We went over and preached kids out of the schools," recalls Reverend Vivian. "The principals locked the doors. At one of the schools, there was a stream of water, and I said, 'Which side are you on? You know, the chilly Jordan is right through here. You've heard it all your life.' Later, when the kids decided they wanted out, they jumped out second-story windows."

After a month of training, the new recruits were ready. D Day was set for May 2. More than a thousand young people were arrested that day as they set out from the Sixteenth Street Baptist Church singing freedom songs. For the first time in history of the movement, the protestors managed literally to fill the jails.

"Once I saw the waves of children going downtown," recollects Shuttlesworth, "and the police couldn't handle it, I knew that the victory was won."

Even more students marched the following day, chanting, "We Want Freedom." King announced, "Yesterday was D Day in Birmingham. Today will be Double D Day." When they were ordered to stop, the youngsters continued marching and chanting. Livid,

Left: *Police dogs and hoses were
turned onto the demonstrators by
order of Eugene "Bull" Connor,
commissioner of public safety.*

Above: *"Bull" Connor.*

Connor ordered fire engines to turn their high-powered hoses on the demonstrators. Knocked to the sidewalks by crushing streams of water, the young people remembered their lessons in nonviolence.

But across the street in Kelly Ingram Park, the fifteen hundred spectators were not all part of King's disciplined, trained, nonviolent army. Angry at the brutal treatment of these children, a few began shouting threats and throwing rocks, bottles, and bricks at policemen. The new developments provoked Bull Connor to abandon whatever was left of his nonviolent pose. The next day newspapers throughout the country and the world carried photographs of dogs biting black children and policemen clubbing prostrate black women.

"Look at 'em run," Bull Connor was heard to say. "Look at those niggers run." But, in fact, most did not run. They stood their ground. When Reverend Shuttlesworth was blasted by high-pressure hoses and injured, Connor told a newsman, "I waited to see Shuttlesworth get his with a hose. I'm sorry I missed it. I wish they'd carried him away in a hearse."

The violence continued. Alabama governor George Wallace promised to "take whatever action I am called upon to take" to preserve law and order. The laws he intended to preserve were Alabama's segregation laws.

"The brutality of the counterforce, as well as the empathy that one felt with the demonstrators, was a critical factor in pulling the attention of the country together," explains former Assistant Attorney General Marshall. "The civil rights movement," President Kennedy later told King with sardonic humor, "owes Bull Connor as much as it owes Abraham Lincoln."

With the mounting pressure of world opinion, the Kennedy administration was finally forced to intervene to seek a truce in Birmingham. As head of the civil rights division of the Justice Department, Marshall was sent to represent the president in negotiations.

King had no intention of easing the pressure until the black people's demands were met. "If the white power structure of this city will meet some of our minimum demands, we will consider calling off the demonstrations," he said. "But we want promises, plus action."

"I went to Birmingham," Marshall explains, "because I knew all those people. I knew Martin King and the SCLC people and Shuttlesworth and the local people. It was a complex situation. Some of them [the whites] wouldn't talk to any blacks at all. Some of them, a few, would talk to local blacks. None of them would talk to Martin

King—the outsiders. So that you had to have a whole series of conversations in order to get anything done. I couldn't communicate with Mr. Conner, but I could communicate with Boutwell as long as we met in the basement closet, so that nobody knew it was going on. You could at least communicate with him.

"What the Justice Department wanted was some move by the city that would recognize the existence of blacks, just recognize that they were people—that was acceptable, that was enough of a move that Martin King and the people with him locally would accept it as being a symbolic recognition of their existence."

King felt that with Marshall as the catalyst the groundwork was laid for an agreement that would ultimately respond to all of the blacks' demands.

The demonstrations and violence continued while the negotiations were taking place. At the height of the campaign, more than twenty-five hundred protestors filled the jails. The police were forced to create holding pens and concentration areas to accommodate all the prisoners. "I'm sure we've had more people to give their witness to freedom by going to jail here in Birmingham than in any city in the United States," proclaimed King. "And with this kind of witness and determination, I am sure that we're going to be able to break down the barriers of segregation." The following day, he added, "Activities which have taken place in Birmingham over the last few days, to my mind, mark the nonviolent movement's coming of age. This is the first time in the history of our struggle that we have been able, literally, to fill the jails."

The same day, May 8, his chief adversary, Bull Connor, said, "We have just started to fight, if that's what they want. We were trying to be nice to them, but they won't let us be nice."

Birmingham's black and white citizens finally reached an agreement on May 10. The city's businessmen pledged to desegregate lunch counters, rest rooms, fitting rooms, and drinking fountains in planned stages within ninety days; to begin upgrading and hiring blacks on a nondiscriminatory basis throughout the industrial community of Birmingham; to cooperate with the movement's legal representative in the release of jailed protestors; and, to prevent the necessity of further demonstrations, to establish a channel of communications between blacks and whites within two weeks of signing.

"These were just little bitty gestures on the part of the city," admits Marshall, "but they were gestures that said for the first time, 'black people are entitled to some respect.' "

As King had insisted it would, militant nonviolence had forced negotiation and, ultimately, an agreement. The demonstrations were halted, but the city's troubles were far from over. The next night, following the announcement of the agreement, a bomb wrecked the house of King's brother, Reverend A. D. King. A second explosion blasted King's headquarters in Room 30 of the Gaston Motel. Fortunately, unbeknownst to the perpetrators, King was in Atlanta that evening.

At the Sunday service at Ebenezer the following morning, King told the congregation, "We have some difficult days ahead, in spite of the agreements made. . . . Tied up in the solution of this problem is the very destiny of this nation. And, if this is not solved, I am convinced that America is doomed and she will lose her moral and political voice because she failed to live up to the great dream of America."

After the bombings, says Marshall, "the state police behaved abominably. They started breaking into black homes and beating people up." The truce was forgotten. Thousands of angry blacks poured into the streets. Fighting ensued. People who had never been part of the nonviolent movement took the bombings as their cue. Despite the urging of men like Wyatt Tee Walker and A. D. King, the enraged blacks burned and looted white establishments.

By the next day, Mother's Day, 250 state troopers had been called into the riot-torn city. President Kennedy told the nation that the federal government intended to protect the agreement. "The Birmingham agreement was and is a fair and just accord," the president told the nation. "It recognized the fundamental right of all citizens to be accorded equal treatment and opportunity. . . . The federal government will not permit it to be sabotaged by a few extremists on either side." He then ordered 3,000 federal troops to stand by at military bases near Birmingham.

"There was some question at the time whether the disorder in the city was so severe that the federal government should use physical force," recalls Marshall. "I was against that, and the reason I was against that was because I knew the army would declare martial law, and if they declared martial law, they would shut up the blacks."

King, feeling that the bombings had been intended to create a violent reaction, set out on his "pool room pilgrimage." He and Abernathy walked into bars and pool halls to plead with young blacks who were not part of the movement to avoid the trap of violence that was being set for them.

*Medgar Evers, NAACP field
secretary, was shot in Jackson,
Mississippi. He was the first civil
rights leader to be assassinated.*

Previous page: **Alabama governor
George Wallace attempted unsuccessfully
to prevent the integration of the
University of Alabama.**

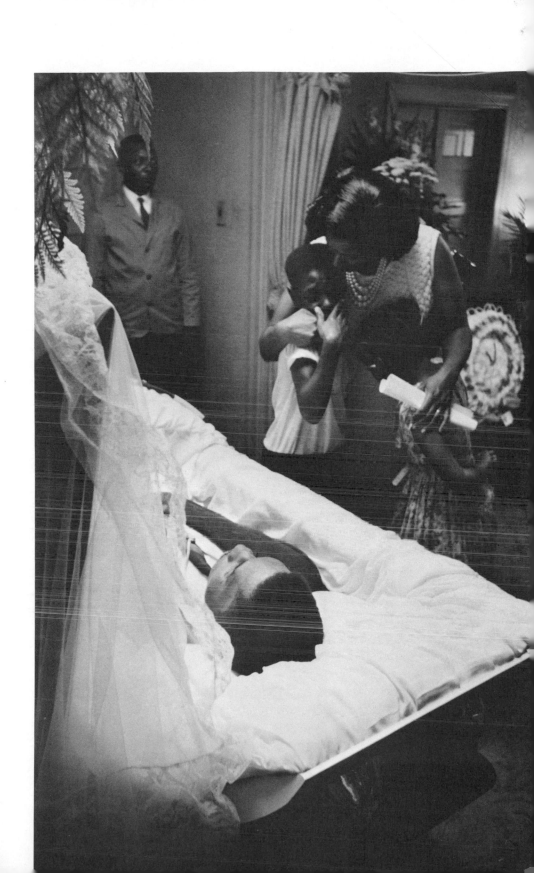

Tensions gradually eased over the next few weeks, and, simultaneously, the Alabama Supreme Court ruled that Connor and the two other city commissioners had no right to remain in office. Connor no longer held power in Birmingham. Boutwell's administration created a climate for steady improvement in Birmingham's race relations.

Project "C" awakened the conscience of the nation. "As far as King's methods were concerned," says Marshall, "I think that they were fitted to the times and the problem. Nothing else would have worked. I think he was absolutely right. The path of nonviolence; the putting the bodies on the line; all of that business of a combination of extraordinary bravery and extraordinary passivity at the same time was exactly right. It evoked, as he knew it would, these brutal reactions from the whites in power, and so you saw these church people being beaten up by thugs—and the thugs were policemen."

"In the end, we accomplished in Birmingham what we set out to do," explains Wyatt Tee Walker. "Birmingham turned loose the forces that gave us the civil rights bill."

On June 11, Alabama's governor George Wallace stood in the "schoolhouse door" in an unsuccessful attempt to prevent the integration of the University of Alabama. In a televised address the same day, President Kennedy told the nation, "We are confronted primarily with a moral issue. It is as old as the Scriptures and it is as clear as the American Constitution. The heart of the question is whether all Americans are to be afforded equal rights and equal opportunities; whether we are going to treat our fellow Americans as we want to be treated.

"One hundred years of delay have passed since President Lincoln freed the slaves, yet their heirs, their grandsons are not fully free. They are not yet freed from the bonds of injustice; they are not yet freed from social and economic oppression. And this nation, for all its hopes and all its boasts, will not be fully free until all its citizens are free.

"We preach freedom around the world, and we mean it. We cherish our freedom here at home. But are we to say to the world—and much more importantly to each other—that this is the land of the free, except for Negroes; that we have no second-class citizens, except for Negroes; that we have no class or caste system, no ghettos, no master race, except with respect to Negroes?

"Now the time has come for this nation to fulfill its promise. The events in Birmingham and elsewhere have so increased the cries for equality that no city or state or legislative body can prudently choose to ignore them.

"I shall ask the Congress of the United States to act, to make a commitment it has not fully made in this century to the proposition that race has no place in American life or law."

King sent the president a telegram, acknowledging the speech as "one of the most eloquent, profound and unequivocal pleas for justice and the freedom of all men ever made by any President."

"Had the Kennedys not been in the White House," says Fred Shuttlesworth, "while King and the others of us were on the street, the country would not now be as committed to human rights nor would people be as concerned as they are."

The following week, Congress was asked to pass the most far-reaching civil rights bill ever proposed by a president. In the opinion of Burke Marshall, "When Kennedy sent down that bill in June 1963, that was to become the 1964 Civil Rights Act, he really put his presidency on the line on civil rights. He didn't go into office believing that his presidency would turn on the issue of civil rights. Why did he do that? He did it because the country just had to have it, and the reason the country had to have it was because of the efficacy of the civil rights movement and especially the work of Martin King."

On the heels of triumph followed tragedy. Hours after President Kennedy's address, Medgar Evers, an NAACP field secretary, was shot to death in Jackson, Mississippi. When he returned to his home shortly after midnight, an assassin lurked in a thicket across the street. As Evers walked toward his door, the blast rang out. Evers was rushed to the hospital, but died almost immediately—the first civil rights leader to be assassinated. Byron de la Beckwith, an ardent segregationist, was indicted for the murder but never convicted.

King said, "This occurrence should cause all persons of good will to be aroused and . . . to be more determined than ever before to break down all of the barriers of racial segregation and discrimination."

With tears streaming down her face, Evers' widow told a crowd of nine hundred people, "Nothing can bring Medgar back, but the cause can live on."

The March on Washington, August 28, 1963.

Chapter Nine

The Dream

I still have a dream. It is a dream deeply rooted in the American dream. I have a dream that one day this nation will rise up and live out the true meaning of its creed, "We hold these truths to be self-evident, that all men are created equal."

MLK, Jr.

AMERICA WAS discovering its conscience. The spring of 1963 marked a turning point in the civil rights movement, and that summer the fervor for freedom spread from the South to the rest of the nation. After the success of Birmingham, Martin King made a triumphant speaking tour to Chicago, Los Angeles, and Detroit, where blacks were rising up to demand "Freedom Now."

King was inspired by the mounting militancy of urban blacks, but he was concerned about the ideological extremism of the black nationalists who were beginning to oppose him. Some denounced King and his nonviolent philosophy as Uncle Tomish. Malcolm X, the articulate champion of the Black Muslims, described the Birmingham action as "an exercise in futility." "What kind of success did they get in Birmingham?" he asked. "A chance to sit at a lunch counter and drink some coffee with a 'cracker'?"

King understood all too well how Malcolm's fiery oratory appealed to blacks in the northern ghettos. "Let the Negro march," he warned whites. "Let him make pilgrimages to city hall. Let him go on freedom rides. And above all, make an effort to understand why he must do this. For if his frustration and despair are allowed to continue piling up, millions of Negroes will seek solace and security in black nationalist ideologies. And this, inevitably, would lead to a frightening racial nightmare."

He was convinced that only nonviolent protest could solve the racial problem. Blacks could never win a violent confrontation, and King felt strongly that victory depended upon moral superiority. "The Negro was willing to risk martyrdom," King wrote in *Why We Can't Wait*, "in order to move and stir the social conscience of his community and the nation. It is not simple to adopt the credo that moral force has as much strength and virtue as the capacity to return a physical blow; or that to refrain from hitting back requires more will and bravery than the automatic reflexes of defense. Yet there is something in the American ethos that responds to the strength of moral force."

In the ten weeks following the Birmingham victory, 758 civil rights demonstrations occurred in 186 cities. The campaign of that summer forced thousands of schools, hotels, restaurants, parks, and swimming pools to desegregate. To capitalize on the momentum, King and the other civil rights leaders joined forces with white labor leaders and clergymen to plan a massive "March on Washington for Jobs and Freedom."

Along with the heads of CORE, SNCC, the NAACP, and the

Urban League, King met with A. Philip Randolph, elder statesman of the civil rights movement and the only black on the executive council of the AFL-CIO, and Walter Reuther, president of the United Auto Workers. Together they laid the groundwork for the march. The committee appointed Bayard Rustin national coordinator for the march. Walter Fauntroy, then head of SCLC's Washington, D.C., bureau, was to be the coordinator in the capital. Hoping for 100,000 participants, the planners urged black and white clergymen to support the project and to involve their congregations. They hoped the march would provide blacks with an opportunity for nonviolent protest and put pressure on Congress to pass Kennedy's civil rights bill.

On June 22, King, Randolph, Farmer, Wilkins, Lewis, and Whitney Young met with President Kennedy to discuss the civil rights bill as well as the idea of the March on Washington. The president was concerned that the march might be ill-timed. It would be counterproductive, he explained, if it provided southern legislators with an excuse to vote against his bill. King reminded him, "Frankly, I have never engaged in any direct-action movement which did not seem ill-timed. Some people thought Birmingham ill-timed." "Including the attorney general," the president quipped.

"In our first meeting with John Kennedy, a week after I was elected chairman of SNCC, he told us he thought the march was a bad idea," recalls John Lewis. "He said it couldn't be controlled. A. Philip Randolph replied, 'Mr. President, there will be a march. The question is what type or form will the march take.' Later, when the administration saw that it was going to happen, they came in, got behind it."

When the meeting came to an end, President Kennedy asked King to stay behind. As they walked in the White House Rose Garden, the president confided that FBI director J. Edgar Hoover was concerned about communist influences on King and the civil rights movement. Hoover charged that there were two known communists on King's staff and had placed King and the SCLC under surveillance. The president said Hoover had named King's long-time advisor Stanley Levison and Jack O'Dell on the SCLC's New York staff. President Kennedy advised the black leader to fire O'Dell and disassociate from Levison. Although he did not actually believe King was influenced by communists, the president knew that any suspicions, however unfounded, about King's associates could discredit the civil rights movement and undermine the administration's pending civil rights bill.

King left the meeting encouraged by the emergence of what he called "a new John F. Kennedy" as a champion of civil rights. But he was deeply disturbed by the allegations against O'Dell and, particularly, Levison, who had been a loyal friend and advisor and had raised a great deal of money for the cause. Reluctantly, he took the president's advice. He asked for O'Dell's resignation and temporarily severed his overt ties with Levison. Eventually, King would restore Levison as an advisor, saying, "There's nothing to hide. And if anybody wants to make something of it, let them try."

The day after his meeting with the president, King led 125,000 people on a great Freedom Walk in Detroit. Introduced as "America's beloved freedom fighter," he called the event "the largest and greatest demonstration for freedom ever held in the United States." "Birmingham tells us something in glaring terms," he told the northern demonstrators. "It says first that the Negro is no longer willing to accept racial segregation in any of its dimensions." Calling segregation a "cancer in the body politic," he continued, "We are through with segregation now, henceforth, and forever." The Freedom Walk in Detroit was in many respects a rehearsal for the upcoming March on Washington.

Planes, trains, buses, and cars began bringing protestors from all over America to the capital on the eve of the march. By midmorning of August 28, the crowd at the base of the Washington Monument had reached ninety thousand. Here the exuberant demonstrators listened to scores of entertainers as they waited for the march to begin. Harry Belafonte, Burt Lancaster, Paul Newman, Sidney Poitier, Charlton Heston, Lena Horne, Sammy Davis, Jr., Marlon Brando, James Baldwin, and Jackie Robinson were among the celebrities who came to lend their support. One hundred and fifty members of Congress also joined demonstrators from across the nation. Folksingers Joan Baez, Peter Paul, and Mary, and Bob Dylan led the crowd in freedom songs. Blacks and whites alike responded to Odetta's bittersweet "If They Ask You Who You Are, Tell Them You're a Child of God."

In the meantime, King and the other black leaders met with President Kennedy, Vice-President Johnson, Secretary of Labor Willard Wirtz, and Burke Marshall. They discussed the urgency of strong civil rights legislation and the prospects for passage of the bill Kennedy had proposed to Congress. John Lewis and many other march organizers felt that the president's bill was both too weak and too late. But the meeting was cordial, and Kennedy said afterward: "One

King and civil rights leaders met with President Kennedy and Vice-President Johnson before the march began.

cannot help but be impressed with the quiet dignity that characterized the thousands who have gathered in the nation's capital from across the country to demonstrate their faith and confidence in our democratic form of government."

The march route covered nearly a mile along the banks of the reflecting pool from the Washington Monument to the Lincoln Memorial. Wave after wave of marchers chanted "We Want Freedom" as they made their way to the memorial. By 1:00 P.M., when singer Camilla Williams officially opened the program with the "Star Spangled Banner," 250,000 people were peacefully assembled. Millions more were watching on television.

The march was a triumph for the nonviolent cause. Before the march began, Rustin had said, "Our aim is to get each marcher to understand fully the significance of why he is there. We are asking each person to be a marshal of himself."

"There was not a single incident," recalls Fauntroy, who felt personally responsible for the success of the march in his own city. "I'll

never forget, I gave them the line, 'Anybody who foments violence is a traitor to the cause. Anybody! You are in the pay of the enemies of civil rights.' "

The spirit was that of a gigantic, friendly picnic. Many carried picket signs; even more carried sandwiches. It was in an atmosphere of amiable chaos that Reverend Fred Shuttlesworth gave the invocation. One by one the civil rights leaders spoke to the crowd and to the nation. Randolph presided, saying, "We are the advance guard of a massive moral revolution for jobs and freedom." He introduced each of the speakers. The rostrum included Whitney Young of the Urban League, Ralph Abernathy, Roy Wilkins of the NAACP, and Dr. Eugene Carson Blake of the National Council of the Churches of Christ of America. Dick Gregory commented wryly, "The last time I saw so many of us together, Bull Connor was doing all the talking."

The audience was particularly moved by the aggressive words of John Lewis, even though Lewis had been asked to tone down his original speech. "I had prepared a speech that I thought really expressed my views and feelings," Lewis remembers. "The night before the march, we were all supposed to make copies of our speeches available to the press committee. Bayard Rustin came and informed me late that night that there was some concern about what I was going to say in the speech. And so there was a meeting. And we made some changes in the speech that night. They said that certain words were inflammatory.

"I wanted to put in there that 'the time may come when we are not going to confine our marching just on Washington, but we might be forced to march through the South, through the heart of Dixie the way Sherman did, pursuing our own policy and burn Jim Crow to the ground, nonviolently, splitting the South into thousands of pieces and putting it back together in the image of democracy.' That was changed.

"And on the whole question of supporting the Kennedy legislation, I said it was too little, too late. I finally said that we supported the proposed legislation, but we supported it with reservations."

Even with the modifications, Lewis delivered an emotionally charged speech: "We are tired!" he bellowed. "We are tired of being beaten by policemen. We are tired of seeing our people locked up in jail over and over again! And then you holler 'Be patient.' How long can we be patient? We want our freedom and we want it now! We do not want to go to jail, but we will go to jail if this is the price

Above: *Congressman Walter Fauntroy, coordinator of the march, remembers being among the group who worked with King on his "I Have a Dream" speech.*

Previous overleaf: *More than 250,000 people joined in the largest demonstration in the history of the civil rights movement.*

we must pay for love, brotherhood and true peace. I appeal to all of you to get in this great revolution which is sweeping this nation—get in and stay in the streets of every city until the revolution of 1776 is completed."

James Farmer was in a Louisiana jail on the day of the march, but he sent a message that was read by his colleague from CORE Floyd McKissick. "We will not stop," he wrote, "until the dogs stop biting us in the South and the rats stop biting us in the North." The program also included sympathetic white speakers, such as Walter Reuther and various clergymen.

The crowd was beginning to thin by late afternoon when Mahalia Jackson's rendition of "I Been 'Buked and I Been Scorned" brought tears to the eyes of the remaining ralliers. Those who departed before Martin King spoke missed the climax of the demonstration.

Each of the speakers had been limited to five minutes. The march organizers had deliberately avoided designating any among them as the keynote speaker. Although each group felt a claim to leadership, the march was a joint effort that transcended personal jealousies.

King had labored on his speech throughout the previous night with his aides Andy Young, Ralph Abernathy, Wyatt Walker, and Walter Fauntroy giving advice. "We wrestled for about four hours," Fauntroy recalls, "because we'd brought drafts of things we ought to be hitting on. I said, 'There's no way in the world you can say what you have to say in five minutes.' That was just a warm up. So finally we just said, 'Well, Martin, you talk to the Lord about it.' "

Thousands applauded when Randolph introduced King as "the moral leader of the nation." King's powerful baritone voice hushed the crowd: "Five score years ago, a great American, in whose symbolic shadow we stand today, signed the Emancipation Proclamation. . . . But one hundred years later, the Negro is still not free."

He began with the words that he and his aides had hammered out the night before, saying America had given the Negro people what amounted to a bad check. "When the architects of our republic wrote the magnificent words of the Constitution and the Declaration of Independence, they were signing a promissory note to which every American was to fall heir. This note was the promise that all men—yes, black men as well as white men—would be guaranteed the unalienable rights of life, liberty, and the pursuit of happiness."

As he spoke, the crowd warmed to him, and he soon departed from his prepared text. Whether his inspiration indeed came from the Lord, or from the enthusiastic throngs, or from the recollection of the dramatic speech he had given in Detroit two months earlier, he changed his thrust. As had happened at so many church services and rallies in the past, his voice invited the crowd not only to listen but also to participate.

"I have a dream," he cried.

"Tell us, tell us," the crowd pleaded.

"I have a dream that one day on the red hills of Georgia, the sons of former slaves and the sons of former slaveowners will be able to sit down together at the table of brotherhood."

"Yes! Yes! I see it," the listeners responded.

He continued improvising, remembering fragments of speeches dating back to 1956. He shared his vision extemporaneously, combining eloquence with spontaneous energy. He spoke to the massive audience as to a congregation, his rhythmic cadence and repetitive phrases building toward the climax.

"I have a dream that my four little children will one day live in a nation where they will be judged not by the color of their skin, but by the content of their character. I have a dream today. I have a dream that one day down in Alabama, with its racists, with its governor dripping in the words of interposition and nullification, one day right there in Alabama, little black boys and black girls will be able to join hands with little white boys and white girls as sisters and brothers.

"I have a dream today!"

"I have a dream that one day 'every valley shall be exalted and every hill and mountain shall be made low. The rough places will be made plain and the crooked places will be made straight, and the glory of the Lord shall be revealed, and all flesh shall see it together.' "

His speech—the most eloquent of his career—was not a well-reasoned legal brief on the civil rights bill, nor an intellectual treatise on the plight of blacks in America. It was a fervent emotional sermon, forged out of the language of Christianity and the spirit of democracy. King's mastery of the spoken word, his personal magnetism, and his sincerity raised familiar platitudes from cliché to commandment. Many wept uncontrollably.

"Let freedom ring," he commanded. "And when this happens, when we allow freedom to ring, when we let it ring from every village and hamlet, from every state and every city, we will be able to speed up that day when all of God's children, black men and

white men, Jews and Gentiles, Protestants and Catholics will be able to join hands and sing in the words of the old Negro spiritual: 'Free at last, free at last, thank God Almighty, we're free at last.' "

The day was a personal victory for King. The orderly conduct of the massive march was an active tribute to his philosophy of non-violence. Equally significant, his speech made his voice familiar to the world and lives today as one of the most moving orations of our time. "I have a dream," he said. And countless millions accepted his dream as their own. "I have a dream," he repeated. And people of all walks life recognized the dreamer as the conscience of an entire nation.

For many, the March on Washington was the apex of the nonviolent civil rights movement. It united black leaders, regardless of the often divergent goals of their organizations. It was the first large-scale participation of whites in the black movement—and the first determined effort by white clergymen. It catapulted King to international prominence. And, of no little importance, it uplifted spirits and morale and encouraged blacks to accelerate their fight for freedom.

"That day, for a moment, it almost seemed that we stood on a height, and could see our inheritance," reminisced author James Baldwin. "Perhaps we could make the Kingdom real, perhaps the beloved community would not forever remain the dream one dreamed in agony."

And then, agony returned. Eighteen days later, in the wake of tumultuous efforts to integrate schools in Alabama, a bomb was tossed into Birmingham's Sixteenth Street Baptist Church while Sunday school was in session. Four little girls were killed as they put on their choir robes, and twenty-one youngsters were injured. "My God, we're not even safe in church," a woman shrieked. King and millions of other Americans were appalled and sickened. "Never in Christian history within a Christian country have Christian churches been on the receiving end of such naked brutality and violence as we are witnessing here in America today," King said. "Not since the days of the Christians in the catacombs has God's house, as a symbol, weathered such an attack as the Negro churches."

Birmingham erupted in violence again. Blacks and whites fought

"Free at last, free at last, thank God Almighty, we're free at last."

in the streets. Crowds became hysterical. Two innocent black teen-agers were shot and killed. Many placed the blame squarely at the feet of Governor George Wallace, who had opposed the court-ordered school desegregation. King could not conceal his anger. "Certainly the Governor of Alabama has to take a great deal of the responsibility for this evil act," he said, "for his defiant, irresponsible words and actions have created the atmosphere for violence and terror all over the state . . . and the murders of yesterday stand as blood on the hands of Governor Wallace."

At the memorial service for the children, novelist John Killens said the tragic bombing marked the demise of nonviolence in the free-dom movement. "Negroes must be prepared to protect themselves with guns," he proclaimed. Christopher McNair, the father of one of the murdered children, disagreed: "What good would Denise have done with a machine gun in her hand?"

Martin King delivered the eulogy, calling the murdered children "martyrs of a holy crusade for human dignity." His hope dominated his anger when he told mourners, "They did not die in vain. God still has a way of wringing good out of evil."

That faith was challenged once again only two months later when a shot rang out in Dallas and struck the heart of America. Martin King was at home in Atlanta when he heard the special bulletin on television. President Kennedy had been shot. Listening to the news, he and Coretta prayed that the young president would live.

And then came the announcement. John F. Kennedy was dead. King turned to his wife and said quietly, "I don't think I'm going to live to reach forty."

"Don't say that, Martin," Coretta pleaded.

But King persisted. "This is what is going to happen to me also."

Grief-stricken, King told reporters, "While the question 'who killed President Kennedy?' is important, the question 'what killed him?' is more important. Our late president was assassinated by a morally inclement climate. It is a climate filled with heavy torrents of false accusation, jostling winds of hatred and raging storms of violence. It is a climate where men cannot disagree without being disagree-able, and where they express their dissent through violence and murder."

Later King struck a sympathetic chord in all Americans when he wrote: "We mourned a man who had become the pride of the nation, but we grieved as well for ourselves because we knew we were sick." (on hearing of death of John F. Kennedy)

Eighteen days after the triumphant march on Washington, a bomb exploded in Birmingham's Sixteenth Street Baptist Church, killing four little girls.

Less than a week after he took office, in his first presidential address to Congress, Lyndon Johnson declared, "No memorial oration or eulogy could more eloquently honor President Kennedy's memory than the earliest possible passage of the civil rights bill for which he fought so long."

Chapter Ten

The Mountaintop

I must confess that there are those moments when I feel a sense of inadequacy as a symbol. It is never easy for one to accept the role of symbolism, without going through constant moments of self-examination. And I must confess that there are moments when I begin to wonder whether I am adequate or whether I am able to face all of the challenges and even the responsibilities of this particular position.

MLK, Jr.

"As I look toward 1964," King wrote in the January issue of the *SCLC Newsletter,* "one fact is unmistakably clear: the thrust of the Negro toward full emancipation will increase rather than decrease." Nineteen sixty-four would be the year when Martin Luther King, Jr.—a man for whom humility was a central aspect of character—would be honored beyond the most fervid imaginings of the most ambitious men. His articulate leadership had awakened the heart and conscience of white America and attracted attention around the world.

On January 3, the newsmagazine *Time* named King "Man of the Year" and featured him on its cover. Haile Selassie was the only other black to have been so honored. In citing him for this honor, *Time* wrote that King had been selected "as a man—but also as a representative of his people for whom 1963 was perhaps the most important year in their history. . . . Few can explain the extraordinary King mystique. Yet he has an indescribable capacity for empathy that is the touchstone of leadership. By deed and by preachment, he has stirred in his people a Christian forbearance that nourishes hope and smothers injustice."

King always accepted his awards and acclaim as a representative of the movement. "I would like to think that my selection . . . was not a personal tribute, but a tribute to the whole freedom movement," he said of the *Time* honor. And the tributes never overshadowed the work that King knew still lay ahead. He was encouraged by President Johnson's strong position on civil rights, and told the *Time* reporter, "He means business. I think we can expect even more from him than we have had up to now. I have implicit confidence in the man, and unless he betrays his past actions, we will proceed on the basis that we have in the White House a man who is deeply committed to help us."

King's confidence was well placed. Under the prodding of President Johnson, the House of Representatives passed a civil rights bill early in 1964. Southerners sent word to the White House that Johnson was going to be "damned sorry" when the November election rolled around, but the southerners in the House were not concerned. They had confidence that the bill would be killed in the Senate.

Early in 1964, King was genuinely surprised when he learned he had been nominated for the world's most prestigious award—the Nobel Peace Prize, which is given annually to the individual or organization who has contributed the most to the "furtherance of peace among men."

In announcing their nomination, eight members of the Swedish Parliament said King was selected because he "had succeeded in keeping his followers to the principle of nonviolence." To be nominated was a tribute in itself. If no one is deemed worthy of the award in a particular year, the prize is not given. His competition was reported to include French president Charles de Gaulle, former president Dwight David Eisenhower, former West German chancellor Konrad Adenauer, and former British prime minister Sir Anthony Eden.

St. Augustine, Florida, not the Nobel Prize, occupied King's thoughts that spring. America's oldest city was almost totally segregated. King had chosen St. Augustine, which was preparing to celebrate its four hundredth birthday, as the focal point for his next campaign, hoping to capitalize on this symbolic event and on the attendant press coverage.

King had a cadre of new associates such as reverends C. T. Vivian and Hosea Williams. He felt their firm and experienced leadership could back up the local movement, which was headed by a courageous black dentist, Dr. R. N. Hayling. "I was the guy that they looked upon as not being able to keep quiet," says Reverend Williams. "I was too impatient. The first thing they did, they sent me to St. Augustine, Florida, and it was really to get me out of circulation. I ended up getting more people in jail in the first two weeks than they had gotten in jail the whole two years the movement had been going."

The action began on Easter Sunday, when nine members of an interracial group of women were arrested for refusing to leave the dining room of the whites-only Monson Motor Court. The protests to desegregate public accommodations received unexpected publicity when one arrested picketer turned out to be Mrs. Malcolm Peabody, mother of the governor of Massachusetts.

"Finally, Dr. King came to St. Augustine," Hosea Williams remembers. "There I really developed greater faith in the man because I saw him do some things. I became SCLC's Castro. I became the tough guy, the nervy guy."

Throughout the next several months, demonstrators participated in a series of sit-ins and night mass marches. The old slave market in the town square became a symbol and a rallying point. The first march took place on May 26, the night of the Florida gubernatorial race. As marchers walked peacefully past the campaign headquarters of Haydon Burns, a segregationist candidate, they heard a bystander say, "If our man's in, you niggers have had it."

Burns was elected. The following night Klansmen armed with iron pipes and chains awaited the marchers at the Slave Market. The first violence erupted on Thursday, May 28, when the marchers knelt to pray. A Klansman shouted, "Niggers ain't got no God," and clubbed a demonstrator. The police moved out of the way, allowing the mob to get through.

King and the protest organizers faced different problems in St. Augustine than they had experienced in other cities. Although the police were not actively hostile, they stood by passively while white segregationists viciously attacked demonstrators. King's forces were battered nightly by local Klansmen. King insisted, nevertheless, that the demonstrations would persist. "We are determined," he exclaimed, "[that] this city will not celebrate its quadricentennial as a segregated city. There will be no turning back."

Addressing a mass meeting in the "ancient city," King praised his nonviolent followers, saying, "I want to commend you for the beauty and the dignity and the courage with which you carried out the demonstrations last week. You confronted the brutality of individuals who feel they can block our righteous efforts toward a just and free society by beating Negroes—and not only Negroes but by beating white people who are here to give objective coverage to what is taking place in this community. But amid all this, you stood up. Soon the Klan will see that all of their violence will not stop us. For we are on our way to Freedom Land, and we don't mean to stop till we get there. . . .

"I got word way out in California," King continued, "that a plot was underway to take my life in St. Augustine, Florida. Well, if physical death is the price I must pay to free my white brothers and all of my brothers and sisters from a permanent death of the spirit, then nothing can be more redemptive. And I'm determined. You see we've long since learned to sing anew with our forefathers of old: 'Before I'll be a slave, I'll be buried in my grave, and go home to my Father, and be saved.' "

King, Abernathy, and sixteen other protestors were arrested and jailed as "unwanted guests," when they staged a stand-in at an exclusive restaurant, overlooking Matanzas Bay.

"I saw Martin do things that truly made my flesh shake on my bones," recalls Hosea Williams. "That's how I really got with him. I began to feel like he was a man who really was living what he

Previous page: *Coretta
Scott King accompanied daughters
Yolanda and Bernice to
hear their father's
Sunday sermon.*

Left: **King with his oldest son,
Martin Luther King, III, after church.**

Next page: **Coretta with
Bunny, Marty, and Yoki.**

Above: **Sunday dinner at the King home.**

preached. I've seen Martin, knowing how bad the Klan wanted him, I've seen him do things no normal man could do."

King remained in prison for two days. While he was imprisoned, Williams made an impassioned speech to demonstrators at the Slave Market while Klansmen stood by. "Negroes have shed blood here that Jack Kennedy shall not have died in vain," he shouted, "and Medgar Evers and the children of Birmingham! Yes, they died and we may die, but we'll die with this in our mind—if the black man loses his freedom, no man will be free. We will bleed and die that America shall be free!"

That evening J. B. Stoner, an Atlanta attorney well known as a defense lawyer for Klansmen, stood in the same spot and proclaimed, "We whites are due more rights, not less. When the Constitution said all men are created equal, it wasn't talking about niggers." He proceeded to lead 170 white marchers, accompanied by state troopers and police dogs, through the black ghetto. When they arrived in the black neighborhood, they were greeted by the sign: "Welcome. Peace and brotherhood to you."

When he was released from jail on nine hundred–dollars bail, King flew directly to Yale University to receive an honorary degree. He was cited by Yale president Kingman Brewster for "eloquence that has kindled the nation's sense of outrage."

Even that eloquence failed to inspire the discouraged demonstrators when King returned to St. Augustine. The St. Augustine crusade was deadlocked. Nowhere had the movement met such brutal defiance by white citizens. "We had a tremendous hospital bill in St. Augustine," recollects Atlanta's Mayor Young, "because they were some of the sickest people we have ever run across. It wasn't the police. It was the Klan, and they organized into what they called the Ancient City Gun Club. But then, they would go by the police headquarters and brag about it afterwards. When I was arrested in St. Augustine and taken into jail, Hoss Manucy, who was the head of the Klan, was sitting on the steps talking to the sheriff. One of the things that happened out of that was that Judge Brian Simpson in Jacksonville exposed the connection between the Klan and the police department in St. Augustine."

King appealed to the president, saying St. Augustine was "the most lawless community he had ever seen." The White House, however, was reluctant to intervene until the Civil Rights Act became law, which would not happen for two weeks.

The unchecked violence reached a peak on June 25, when eight hundred Klansmen, deployed by Hoss Manucy, attacked an SCLC demonstration. They tore the clothes off a thirteen-year-old black girl and mauled a *Newsweek* reporter who stepped in to protect her. The following day, Governor Farris Bryant banned the night marches, risking a federal contempt of court charge. Without support from Washington, the SCLC was stalemated.

When the governor finally made some attempts to establish a biracial negotiating committee, a disheartened King closed down his headquarters, hoping that President Johnson's signing of the civil rights bill would improve the situation in St. Augustine.

Thirty days later, Dr. Hayling, the dentist who had been leading the movement in St. Augustine for years, went to court and sued the city of St. Augustine for denying blacks their civil rights. This time he won. White businessmen and local politicians saved face by declaring, "Everybody must abide by the law whether we like it or not." King proclaimed a victory. But, in fact, he left St. Augustine much as he found it.

His distress was offset to a degree by the passage of the Civil Rights Act of 1964. King and other civil rights leaders were invited to the White House on July 2 to watch President Johnson sign the bill into law. The new law, said President Johnson, "does not give special treatment to any citizen." It does, however, say that "those who are equal before God shall now also be equal in the polling booths, in the classrooms, in the factories, and in hotels and restaurants and movie theatres, and other places that provide service to the public." King applauded the bill as an act of "good faith," but for many black Americans, freedom was coming too slowly.

Some blacks, particularly those in the ghettos of the urban North, had become disenchanted with King and his nonviolent philosophy. But a poll taken by *Newsweek* magazine showed that 88 percent of all blacks and 95 percent of the black leaders regarded King as the most successful spokesman for their race. Although King continued to defend his policy of nonviolence—"I think it is possible to be militantly nonviolent"—he understood the growing impatience of black people. "I think the greatest disappointment is the slow pace of the progress," he told reporters. Nor was he surprised when the nation's ghettos erupted in flames during the summer of 1964: "Until the Harlems and racial ghettos of our nation are destroyed and the Negro is brought into the mainstream of American life, our beloved nation will be on the verge of being plunged into the abyss of social disruption," he warned. Nevertheless, King deplored the violence.

"Lawlessness, looting, and violence cannot be condoned whether used by the racists or the reckless of any color," he said, hoping to dissuade ghetto residents from a violent course.

The rioting might have been even worse that summer, had it not been for King's calming influence. But he was being assailed from both sides, by those who felt he was moving too fast and by those who denounced him for moving too slowly.

As the summer Democratic and Republican conventions approached, King was more convinced than ever that the time had come to move the struggle from the streets into the voting booth. Without the ballot, blacks would forever have to "vote with their feet." In November, the nation would elect a president, and King knew that the black vote could be an important factor. He strongly supported the Mississippi Project—a major campaign to register blacks in that state, where thousands had never voted—in hopes of sending a black delegation to the Democratic convention.

Andrew Goodman and Michael Schwerner, two white members of CORE, and their guide, James Chaney, a black Mississippi civil rights worker, were among those who went to Mississippi to register voters. In June, they were arrested for speeding in Philadelphia, Mississippi. That was the last time they were seen alive. Sheriff Lawrence Rainey and his deputy, Cecil Price, claimed the men had been held for six hours and then released. When the men were not found, President Johnson sent 210 Navy men to search the area and ordered the FBI to make a full inquiry. The search was still going on when King arrived in Mississippi to assist the voter registration campaign.

In August, the bodies of the three civil rights workers were found buried in a nearby dam. When the nation learned of the killings, hundreds of civil rights workers rushed to Mississippi and neighboring states to pursue the mission of the three martyred young men.

Murder is a state offense. The Mississippi courts took no legal action against the accused murderers. In fact, Sheriff Rainey and Deputy Price became local heroes. Eventually, Rainey, Price, and sixteen others, including the Imperial Wizard of the Ku Klux Klan, were indicted by a federal grand jury for conspiring to deprive the murdered men of their constitutional rights to life and liberty. Much later, Price and six other conspirators were found guilty. It was the first time a Mississippi jury had returned a "guilty" verdict in a civil rights murder case. Rainey was acquitted.

Although the voter registration campaign in Mississippi was a success, the civil rights movement sustained staggering casualties that

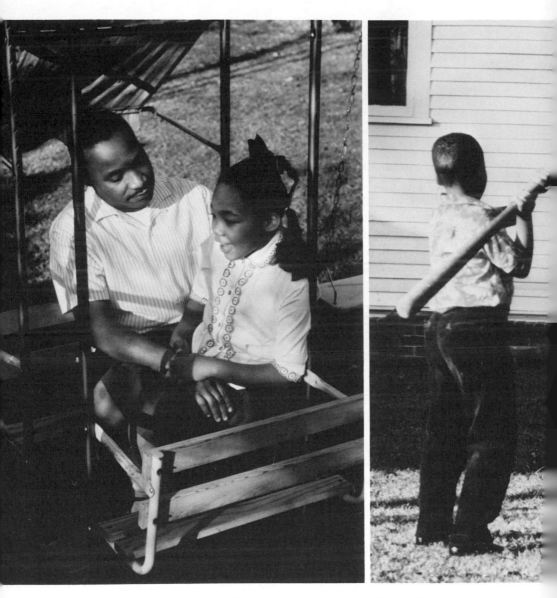

Shared moments with Yolanda . . .   *Martin III . . .*

and Dexter Scott.

King with daughter Bernice.

King is congratulated by King Olav V of Norway upon becoming the third black, twelfth American, and youngest person ever to win the Nobel Peace Prize.

summer. "People were bitter, frustrated, torn-apart, battle-fatigued, and everything else," says John Lewis. Six people had been killed, eighty beaten, more than a thousand arrested. Thirty-seven Negro churches and thirty-one black homes had been bombed.

Near exhaustion himself, King was in the hospital in Atlanta for a check-up and rest on October 14, when he learned he had won the Nobel Peace Prize. "For a while, I thought it was a dream, and then I realized it was true!" he said. "I'm glad people in other nations are concerned with our problems here."

Martin Luther King, Jr., became the third black, the twelfth American, and the youngest person ever to receive the award instituted by Alfred Nobel in 1895. It was the dramatic climax of a year that had witnessed the passage of a far-reaching civil rights bill, devastating riots in northern ghettos, stalemate in St. Augustine, and the tragic murder of three civil rights workers in Mississippi.

Congratulatory calls and telegrams came from all over the country and the world. Reporters and photographers swarmed to King's hospital room. "This is an extremely moving moment in my life," he told them. "The notice that I have received the 1964 Nobel Prize for Peace is as great a shock for me as was the news of my nomination some months ago. It fills me with deep humility and gratitude to know that I have been chosen as the recipient of this foremost of earthly honors."

Dr. Ralph Bunche, the only other black American to have won the prize, expressed the sentiments of many, saying, "This announcement by the Nobel Peace Prize Committee is a striking international recognition of the cause and struggle of the American Negro for full equality in the American society and for full participation in the mainstream of American life."

Not everyone agreed. "They're scraping the bottom of the barrel when they pick him," said Bull Connor. "He's caused more strife and trouble in this country than anyone I can think of." An irate J. Edgar Hoover fumed, "He was the last person in the world who should ever have received it." Antagonized by King's criticism of the FBI, Hoover went on to call King "the most notorious liar in the country."

King's family, closest friends, and associates accompanied him to Oslo, Norway, for the Nobel presentation. On the way, they stopped in London, where King preached at St. Paul's Cathedral—the only non-Anglican to preach there in the church's 291-year history. From the pulpit, he donated the entire fifty-four thousand–dollar Nobel

Prize to the black movement—to all of those who in his opinion deserved equal recognition.

The first night in Oslo, Daddy King could not suppress the pride he took in his son's achievement. "I always wanted to make a contribution, and all you got to do if you want to contribute, you got to ask the Lord, and let Him know, and the Lord heard me and in some special kind of way I don't even know, He came down through Georgia and He laid His hand on me and my wife and He gave us Martin Luther King and our prayers were answered and when my head is cold and my bones are bleached the King family will go down not only in American history but in world history because Martin King is a Nobel Prize-winner."

Hundreds of cheering Norwegians greeted the Kings at the Oslo airport. The largest audience ever to witness the Peace Prize ceremonies crowded into Festival Hall of the University of Oslo on the morning of the presentation. King received the award with characteristic humility. "I accept the Nobel Prize for Peace at a moment when twenty-two million Negroes of the United States are engaged in a creative battle to end the long night of racial injustice. I accept this award on behalf of the civil rights movement which is moving with determination and a majestic scorn for risk and danger to establish a reign of freedom and a rule of justice.

"I am mindful that only yesterday in Birmingham, Alabama, our children, crying out for brotherhood, were answered with fire hoses, snarling dogs, and even death," he continued. "I am mindful that only yesterday in Philadelphia, Mississippi, young people seeking to secure the right to vote were brutalized and murdered. Therefore I must ask why this prize is awarded to a Movement which is beleaguered and committed to unrelenting struggle; to a Movement which has not won the very peace and brotherhood which is the essence of the Nobel Prize. After contemplation I conclude that this award, which I receive on behalf of the Movement, is a profound recognition that nonviolence is the answer to the crucial political and racial questions of our time—the need for man to overcome oppression without resorting to violence."

Overnight, King became an international leader—a symbol of world peace. He knew that if the Nobel Prize was to mean anything, he must commit himself more than ever to attaining the goals of the black movement through peace. "I have been to the mountaintop," he told a packed Negro church in Harlem on his return from Stockholm. "I really wish I could stay on the mountain; but I must go

back to the valley. I must go back, because my brothers and sisters down in Mississippi and Alabama are sweltering under the heat of injustice. There are people starving in the valley, and people who don't have jobs, and people who can't vote. . . . There are those who need hope. There are those who need to find a way out. . . . Oh, I say to you tonight, my friends, I'm not speaking as one who's never seen the burdens of life. I've had to stand so often amid the chilly winds of adversity, staggered by the jostling winds of persecution. I've had to stand so often amid the surging murmur of life's restless sea. But I go back with a faith. . . . And I *still* have a dream."

On his way back to Atlanta, King stopped in Washington, D.C., to meet with President Johnson and urge him to push a voting rights bill through Congress. The president expressed his determination to secure the right to vote for every American citizen, but told King he was not optimistic about Congress passing a voting bill on the heels of the new Civil Rights Act. King knew that if southern blacks wanted to vote, they would have to write yet another bill on the streets.

King, with civil rights leaders and members of Congress, witnessed the signing of the Civil Rights Act of 1964 by President Lyndon B. Johnson.

Demonstrators came from all over the country to join the protest in Selma, Alabama.

Chapter Eleven

Return to the Valley

*We must gain political power, and we must
come to the point of being able to participate in
government. No longer must we be willing to be
disenfranchised. We must say, "Give us the ballot."
We are determined to have the ballot, and we are
determined to have it now.*

MLK, Jr.

EVEN AS MARTIN KING was accepting the Nobel Peace Prize, plans were underway for his "return to the valley" in Selma, Alabama. The SCLC's campaign to register voters in Alabama's Black Belt was to usher in the new year—1965. King believed that the ultimate foundation of black people's power was the ballot. With the vote, they could begin to control their own destinies.

"All through his life, every time we were demonstrating, we also registered voters," explains Andrew Young. "He saw that the United States would never deal with its racism and its militarism or its economic exploitation of the poor, whatever color they might be, until the one party racist politics of the South was broken. He said, as far back as 1957, if you give us the ballot, we will elect men of good will to the legislatures."

"We had dealt in Montgomery with transportation, dealt in Birmingham and St. Augustine with public accommodations," explains Hosea Williams, the SCLC's national program director at that time. "So we decided after a long three- or four-hour session that the next move was the franchise, voter registration."

Selma was the perfect target. The town's 15,000 blacks were a slight majority of the total population. Yet there were only 350 registered black voters. For the past eighteen months, the Student Nonviolent Coordinating Committee had been trying to register voters in Selma.

"We found out SNCC had been driven out of Selma," says Williams. "It came out that the man [Sheriff] Jim Clark in Selma, he won't even let black folks meet. Anytime four or more people get together, they are arrested. Jim Clark even sent deputies into churches where people would be having worship service, to see whether they were serving God or whether they were talking civil rights."

"Selma was kind of like South Africa," says Young. "No public meetings were allowed; no more than three people could walk down the street at the same time."

When SCLC decided to focus its upcoming campaign in Selma, SNCC chairman John Lewis says, "people in SNCC resented it from the very outset. But we couldn't say to SCLC and couldn't say to Dr. King, 'You don't come to Selma.' " Many of the younger black leaders had taken to calling King "De Lawd." Julian Bond, now a Georgia senator, was an official of SNCC when he complained that King had "sold the concept that one man will come to your town and save you."

"We are going to start a march on the ballot boxes by the thousands," King told seven hundred blacks at Brown's Chapel Methodist Church as he initiated the Selma campaign. "We must be willing to go to jail by the thousands. We are not asking, we are demanding the ballot."

"Dr. King kept saying that the goal was to get Selma to write a Voting Rights Act of 1965 as Birmingham had written the Civil Rights Act of 1964," recalls Lewis. "In Selma we had to really pull out everything that we had, to stay there until the country was aroused and the conscience of white America was pricked."

The first days of the demonstration were peaceful. Selma's white population had learned a lesson from Montgomery and Birmingham. Aware that brutality would only induce sympathy for the protestors, white residents, under the leadership of Mayor Joe Smitherman and the commissioner of public safety, Captain J. Wilson Baker, planned to ignore the action. But almost immediately, antagonism developed between Police Chief Baker and County Sheriff James G. Clark, who was in command at the Dallas County Courthouse, where voter registration was to take place.

"I remember the first time Dr. King came into Selma," says John Lewis. "It was January 18, 1965, and we went down on a mass march, hundreds of people, to the courthouse and stood in a very orderly fashion. Sheriff Clark met us, and he said to me: 'John Lewis, you are nothing but an agitator. You're the lowest form of humanity.' "

That day, Captain Baker watched silently as King became the first black to register as a guest in the hundred-year-old Albert Hotel and to eat in a white restaurant in Selma. But Sheriff Clark disagreed with Baker's methods. He ordered the police commissioner to send home the crowd lined up to register to vote at the courthouse. One King staff member quipped, "Jim Clark is another Bull Connor. We should put him on the staff."

Throughout January and February, there were a series of marches and confrontations in Selma that resulted in dozens of arrests. The protests centered around the voter registration lines at the courthouse. Blacks would stand in line for hours waiting to register, only to be told the office was closed, "Come back another day." Occasionally, they would be allowed to fill out the forms, but their applications would be thrown out on a technicality. In some nearby towns, a prospective voter was required to have two registered voters to vouch for him. Since no blacks were registered, and no whites would vouch for a black, no one could vouch for the would-be voters.

*Twenty years later, Reverend Hosea Williams
remembers leading the first march
across the Edmund Pettus Bridge with
John Lewis of SNCC.*

Al Lingo, director of public safety, commanded the state troopers to block the path of the marchers.

On February 2, King and Abernathy planned to lead 265 protestors from Brown's Chapel to the courthouse to protest the slow pace at which registrars were enrolling black voters. At a mass meeting the night before, King preached a nonviolent course: "I do come to tell you tonight that violence may win a temporary victory, but it cannot win permanent peace."

As the protestors gathered, King tried to explain the purpose of their march. "For the past month, the Negro citizens of Selma, Alabama, and Dallas County have been attempting to register by the hundreds. To date, only fifty-seven persons have entered the registrar's office, while two hundred and eighty have been jailed. Of the fifty-seven who have attempted to register, none have received notice of successful registration. . . . Now we must call a halt to these injustices."

"We are getting ready to move to the courthouse," King continued. "We're all going together today. We're going to walk together. We're going to walk together because we're not parading. We will obey every traffic law, every traffic signal we will stop for; we will not stand in the way of egress and ingress. We will not do anything to block the orderly process of movement in the community. We feel that we need to join together and move on to the courthouse."

They had walked about three blocks when Captain Baker stopped them, saying, "This is a deliberate attempt to violate this city's parade ordinance. You will have to break up into small groups."

"We don't feel we're disobeying any law," King replied. "We feel we have a constitutional right to walk down to the courthouse." Baker arrested the entire party for marching without a parade permit.

The arrest of the Nobel laureate made worldwide headlines. Most of the marchers were released on bail, but knowing the publicity would help their cause, King and Abernathy chose to remain in jail for five days. From his jail cell King wrote, "This is Selma, Alabama. There are more Negroes in jail with me than there are on the voting rolls."

While King remained in jail, militant black leader Malcolm X arrived in Selma at the invitation of SNCC. Speaking to the crowd at Brown's Chapel, Malcolm X emphasized the necessity of answering violence with violence. But he later told Coretta King privately, "I want Dr. King to know that I didn't come to Selma to make his job difficult. I really did come thinking that I could make it easier. If the white people realize what the alternative is, perhaps they will be more willing to hear Dr. King." Two weeks later, Malcolm was assassinated at the Audubon Ballroom in New York City.

When a group of 165 children staged a protest demonstration on February 10, Sheriff Clark and his deputies encircled the youngsters inside a cordon of trucks and cars and herded them out of town. The caravan moved at a rapid pace into the surrounding countryside, forcing the children to trot. Sobbing and out of breath, many of the youngsters fell behind. Some of those who could not keep up were prodded by snickering deputies. "You kids want to march," one taunted, "We'll give you a good march."

National interest in the Selma campaign had begun to flag, but on February 18, Jimmie Lee Jackson, a twenty-six-year-old black man, was fatally shot by state troopers during a demonstration in Marion, Alabama, only thirty miles from Selma. A number of black demonstrators were viciously beaten.

To protest what had happened to Jimmie Jackson, King and the SCLC proposed a march from Selma to Montgomery, where they would take their cause before Governor George Wallace. King warned his followers at Brown's Chapel, "I can't promise you that it won't get you beaten." Wallace issued an order prohibiting the march and commanded state troopers to take "whatever steps are necessary" to stop it.

By this time, the rivalry between the SCLC and SNCC had reached major proportions. "We had a meeting in Atlanta in the basement of a little black restaurant," remembers John Lewis. "We met for hours on the night of March 6, 1965. SCLC had announced a march from Selma to Montgomery. SNCC people said, 'We don't want to march. Just too many people are going to get killed in it.' There was a whole argument about Dr. King getting people hurt and leaving. I took the position as chairman of SNCC, and as an individual really, that the people of Alabama wanted to march; they had a right to march; and I was going to go and march with them. Whether the SNCC organization made this decision or not, I'm from Alabama, I grew up ninety miles from Selma, and I was going. Stokely [Carmichael] and [James] Forman and others said we shouldn't support the march, but if we wanted to march as individuals, we should."

Two days later, nearly six hundred marchers met at Brown's Chapel. Equipped with food, bedrolls, and blankets, they prepared to make the fifty-four mile march to the state capitol in Montgomery. Martin King did not march. Some say his associates persuaded him not to lead this march because they were anticipating violence; some claim there had been threats against his life; still others argued that King was needed out of jail to raise funds and oversee the action. "We never thought anything would happen like it did," insists Lewis. "We thought we would just be arrested."

King's field general—Hosea Williams—took the lead, marching beside Lewis. "I was prepared to walk and march with the people there, go to jail with them, and I felt I should be there with those six hundred people," says Lewis, "but SNCC as an organization said, 'We will have nothing to do with it.'"

The march began quietly, as the protestors set out in pairs. They traveled the first six blocks to Broad Street without incident. As they turned to the Edmund Pettus Bridge, which would take them to Highway 80 and Montgomery, the marchers passed a small posse of armed volunteers led by Sheriff Clark. Across the bridge, access to Highway 80 was blocked by state troopers standing shoulder to

Previous overleaf: *The marchers were assaulted and teargassed by troopers when they reached the base of the bridge.*

Above: *King met with Reverend Hosea Williams, James Forman of SNCC, Reverend Abernathy, and James Farmer of CORE to discuss strategy the day after the beatings on the Edmund Pettus Bridge.*

Reverend C. T. Vivian of the SCLC attempted to convince Police Chief
Wilson Baker to allow the demonstrators to march to Montgomery.

shoulder. "When we got to the apex of the bridge," recalls Reverend Frederick D. Reese of Selma, the first black candidate for mayor
of Selma, "we saw a sea of blue—blue uniforms, blue helmets and
patrol cars." As the marchers moved forward, they could see the
troopers don their gas masks.

When the first marchers were within fifty feet of the state troopers,
the major in charge ordered them to halt. Williams asked the major,
"May we have a word with you?" "There's not going to be any
talking today," the commanding officer replied. "You're going to
take those niggers back to that church." Calling through a bullhorn,
the state trooper gave the marchers three minutes to turn back and

disperse. Instead, in a classic Gandhian action, they knelt on the pavement. Within moments the troopers advanced with nightsticks, bull whips, and tear gas, forcing the unarmed marchers to retreat back across the bridge.

"It was like a battle zone: all those people choking in the gas, being hit and beaten," recalls Lewis, whose own skull was fractured in the melee. Marchers ran coughing, crying, and even vomiting through the cloud of tear gas. One black woman screamed, "Please, no! God, we're being killed." Across the street, white spectators cheered. A trooper intentionally dropped a tear gas grenade beside a black woman who had been beaten into semiconsciousness.

Clark's posse was waiting on the Selma side of the bridge to add their force to the already unequal struggle, driving the helpless demonstrators, beaten and bleeding, back to Brown's Chapel. In town, Captain Baker moved between the clashing groups, holding off Sheriff Clark and his posse and persuading the blacks to return to the church. More than sixty marchers were treated for injuries at the parsonage, where emergency facilities were quickly set up. Seventeen others were taken to the hospital with more serious injuries. His head spinning from the blows, John Lewis told the returning marchers, "Next time we march, we may have to keep going when we get to Montgomery. We may have to go on to Washington."

Within hours, news of the beatings in Selma spread around the world. People everywhere were horrified by what they saw on their television screens. Newspaper headlines called it "Bloody Sunday." King announced that he and Abernathy would lead another march from Selma to Montgomery on March 9 and asked American clergymen—black and white—to join the Selma march.

On March 8, the United States Federal Court issued a temporary injunction against the upcoming march. President Johnson publicly asked King to postpone it. But already more than four hundred priests, ministers, and rabbis had arrived in Selma in response to King's call, ready to participate in the next day's march. "It's better to die on the highway than make a butchery of my conscience. I'd better go through with it," King declared, knowing he would be in violation of the court injunction.

President Johnson sent former Florida governor LeRoy Collins, head of the Federal Community Relations Service, to Selma to help keep the peace. Collins suggested a compromise march to the bridge, where the demonstrators would pray, then turn around and return to the church. This plan would not violate the injunction because the marchers would not leave the Selma city limits. Sheriff Clark, whose previous actions had been severely criticized, agreed to the march plan and promised to control his men.

King, too, felt the new terms would provide a face-saving alternative for both sides, although he admitted to only his closest associates that he had compromised the march and did not intend to go all the way to Montgomery.

Before departing the following day, King led nine hundred demonstrators in prayer. "The only way we can really achieve freedom is to somehow conquer the fear of death," he said. "But if a man has not discovered something that he will die for, he isn't fit to live. . . . We've gone too far to turn back now. We must let them know that nothing can stop us—not even death itself. We must be ready for a season of suffering."

Fifteen hundred marchers, including at least 450 clergymen from all over the country, followed the identical route from Brown's Chapel to the Pettus Bridge. Again they were greeted by troopers, but no one reached for a club or a canister of tear gas. As if to lure the demonstrators toward the Montgomery highway, the law officers opened their barricade. King led the people in prayer and then told them to turn around and go back. Few understood; many felt betrayed; but every demonstrator obeyed, and the march ended without violence.

John Lewis agreed with King's decision. "James Forman and the people from SNCC were insisting that the people should continue to march," says Lewis. "Break through that police line. I think it's very much in keeping with the philosophy of nonviolence to retreat—to make a stand, back off, and come back another day."

Within hours the peace was shattered. After eating dinner in a black-operated restaurant, three white Unitarian ministers were brutally beaten by four white men exclaiming, "You want to know what it's like to be a real nigger." Reverend James Reeb, whose skull had been crushed with a two-by-four, died without ever regaining consciousness.

The next day, seventy priests and nuns from Chicago arrived in Selma to protest the slaying. Archbishop Iakovos of the Greek Orthodox church led an ecumenical memorial service for the slain minister. During the tribute, King said, "Our nation will recognize its real heroes; they will be thousands of dedicated men and women with a noble sense of purpose that enables them to face jeering and hostile mobs. . . . One day the South will know that when these

Dallas County Sheriff Jim Clark (center).

dedicated children of God courageously protested segregation, they were in reality standing up for the best in the American dream."

Chief Baker apprehended three of Reverend Reeb's four assailants; all were members of the Ku Klux Klan.

That same evening, President Johnson addressed a rare joint session of Congress, making a strong commitment to the black cause. "I speak tonight for the dignity of man and the destiny of democracy," he told Congress and the nation. "At times history and fate meet at a single time in a single place to shape a turning point in man's unending search for freedom. So it was a century ago at Appomattox. So it was last week in Selma, Alabama. . . . What happened in Selma is part of a far larger movement which reaches into every section and state of America. It is the effort of American Negroes to secure for themselves the full blessings of American life. Their cause must be our cause too. It is not just Negroes, but all of us, who must overcome the crippling legacy of bigotry and injustice." And then, in his familiar southern drawl, he concluded, *"And we shall overcome!"* The president then promised to submit a bill to Congress that would guarantee voting rights to all citizens and assigned it first priority. There was little doubt that Congress would pass the bill. America was demanding it.

The same day, a federal court overruled the city of Selma's ban on demonstrations. The thoughtful decision by United States district judge Frank Johnson was, according to Burke Marshall, not by the letter of the law, but by the spirit of the law. "The march blocked traffic. It did cause traffic jams," explains Marshall. "It is not the kind of demonstration that would normally be constitutionally protected. Johnson explained in his decision that he was measuring the kind of demonstration against the enormity of the wrongs being protested against. He knew many of the wrongs that were being protested against by the marchers in Selma, which included police brutality, enormous systematic racial oppression, and denial of any right to the ballot. And measured against these wrongs, he thought the tactics that Martin King was leading justified, not only morally, and not only in some theoretical system of justice, but legally and constitutionally. And I think he was right about that."

The Selma movement dragged on. After two murders and nearly thirty-eight hundred arrests, only about fifty blacks had been registered to vote. In nearby Montgomery, James Forman of SNCC led six hundred protestors in a march on the county courthouse. Five state troopers and ten sheriff's possemen on horseback rushed the crowd, injuring eight demonstrators. Forman called for massive direct action to test President Johnson's sincerity, proposing that the black community "tie up every bus, every street, and commit every act of civil disobedience ever seen." Taking the rostrum after Forman, King suggested instead a peaceful "all-out" demonstration on the Montgomery County Courthouse the next day. Forman agreed to King's proposal.

Police provided protection as sixteen hundred marchers walked to the courthouse the next day. It had been almost exactly nine years since King was arrested at the same courthouse and taken to jail. King told the demonstrators, "We are here today because we do not like what happened in Montgomery yesterday. We are here to say to the white man that we will no longer let them use their clubs on us in the dark corners. We're going to make them do it in the glaring light of television."

King announced that a federal judge had ruled "that we have a legal and constitutional right to march from Selma to Montgomery." As protestors prepared for another march from Selma to Montgomery, Governor Wallace claimed he was unable to promise protection for the marchers, so President Johnson federalized the National Guard. "Over the next several days, the eyes of the nation will be upon Alabama," the president told newsmen, "and the eyes of the world will be upon America."

The five-day march from Selma to Montgomery finally began on March 21. Before leaving Brown's Chapel, King spoke to the crowd: "Because of the system we don't have much education, and some of us don't know how to make our nouns and verbs agree. But thank God we have our bodies, our feet and our souls."

Two weeks after the rout on Edmund Pettus Bridge, King led more than three thousand marchers, including clergymen and women from throughout the United States, safely along the identical march route. According to the judge's ruling, only three hundred marchers were to be allowed to continue after the first eight miles. Sheriff Clark stood by quietly, wearing a button in his lapel that read "Never"—his answer to the blacks' plea for "Freedom Now."

Thousands and thousands of demonstrators from all over the country arrived in Montgomery to join the three hundred pilgrims as they completed their fifty-four-mile trek. Nearly twenty-five thousand people converged on the state capitol, joining in the chorus of "We Shall Overcome." Although Governor Wallace refused to speak to the marchers, their enthusiasm was not diminished. Civil rights

*Troopers maintained a human roadblock to prevent
the marchers from proceeding to Montgomery.*

"We've gone too far to turn back now,"
said King. "We must let them know that
nothing can stop us—not even death itself.
We must be ready for a season of suffering."

After two weeks of waiting, marchers learned that Judge Frank Johnson had ruled that the march from Selma to Montgomery could continue.

leaders and entertainers congratulated them on their bravery. "Today," declared King, "I want to tell the city of Selma, today I want to say to the state of Alabama, today I want to say to the people of America and the nations of the world that we are not about to turn around. We are on the move now. Yes, we are on the move and no wave of racism can stop us. And the burning of our churches will not divert us. . . . We are on the move now. Like an idea whose time has come, not even the marching of mighty armies can halt us. We're moving to the land of freedom."

As evening approached, volunteers drove the marchers back to Selma. One such driver was Mrs. Viola Liuzzo, a white woman from Detroit and the mother of five. She had driven one carload to Selma and was on her way back to Montgomery with her nineteen-year-old black guide to pick up another group when gunfire shattered her car window. Viola Liuzzo was killed.

Four members of the Ku Klux Klan were arrested for the murder.

On the road to Montgomery, King and the marchers were protected by the National Guard.

President Johnson condemned the Klan on nationwide television. Mrs. Liuzzo, he said, "was murdered by enemies of justice, who for decades have used the rope and the gun, the tar and the feathers to terrorize their neighbors. They struck by night . . . for their purposes cannot stand the light of day." Although the men were never convicted of murder, a state offense, because no state authority took action, they were eventually convicted by the Montgomery Federal District Court of conspiring to violate the rights of persons taking part in the civil rights march. They were sentenced to the maximum of ten years imprisonment.

Selma, Martin King later told the press, "did more to dramatize the indignities and the injustices that Negro people continue to face in the state of Alabama and many other sections of the South. I think it was the most powerful and dramatic civil rights protest that

Previous page: *King met with President Johnson to discuss the new Voting Rights Act.*

Above: *Segregationists used intimidation tactics to try to prevent blacks from exercising their right to register and vote.*

has ever taken place in the South, and I think it well justified the cost that we put in it."

The politics of the American South changed forever on August 6, 1965. On that day, President Johnson signed the new Voting Rights Act. The new law potentially opened the voting booth to two and a half million previously disenfranchised southern blacks. It empowered the attorney general to send federal registrars into counties where there was evidence of discrimination, and it abolished poll taxes, literacy tests, and other prerequisites that had been used to disqualify black voters.

"What happened in Selma that day was the high point of the civil rights movement," says Lewis, who was elected to the Atlanta city council in 1982. "After Selma, the South and the American political system were never the same again."

The James Meredith March against Fear.

Chapter Twelve

We Have a Power

Many of the young people proclaiming Black Power today were but yesterday the devotees of black-white cooperation and nonviolent direct action. . . . If they are America's angry children today, this anger is not congenital. It is a response to the feeling that a real solution is hopelessly distant because of the inconsistencies, resistance and faintheartedness of those in power.

MLK, Jr.

KING UNDERSTOOD that the Voting Rights Act would be meaningless without a strong campaign to educate and register black voters throughout the South. Accordingly, he announced that the SCLC would organize an all-out registration drive under the direction of Hosea Williams. The campaign would concentrate on 120 rural counties across the South where blacks comprised at least 40 percent of the population. By the time the bill was finally signed, fifteen hundred volunteers from all over the country had spread into the Black Belt counties of Alabama, Georgia, Mississippi, North and South Carolina, and Florida.

In areas such as Dallas, Perry, Wilcox, and Greene counties in Alabama it became necessary to request federal referees to help enforce the law. In other regions, the simple fact that the bill was now law made it possible to negotiate with state officials without requesting federal assistance. In Alabama, Mississippi, and Louisiana, federal examiners immediately opened offices in fourteen counties. In a single day, they registered more than a thousand new voters.

The greatest gains in voter registration occurred in Alabama, where the most federal employees had been dispatched and where for several years King and his staff had concentrated their People to People tours to educate voters. SCLC volunteers patiently explained the voting procedures and organized public forums where blacks could meet and hear local candidates.

Although much remained to be accomplished, the early statistics were impressive. In the seven months following the bill's passage, more than 300,000 black voters were registered for the first time. In the same period, all but four southern states had registered more than 50 percent of their eligible black voters. King also maintained constant pressure on President Johnson for increasingly forceful implementation of the Voting Rights Act, and the nation began to witness the growing influence of the southern black on politics.

The Alabama primary elections of 1966 demonstrated both the new strength and the residual weakness of black voting power. Fifty-two black candidates filed for county or legislative offices in the Alabama primary. Although none won outright, twenty-four survived to the primary run-off, and four were ultimately victorious. The black vote also brought victory for many white candidates who were racial moderates. In Dallas County, for example, segregationist sheriff Jim Clark was defeated by moderate Wilson Baker.

In early June, at the same time King was broadening his People

to People tours to include northern ghettos, James Meredith, who
had been the first black student to enter the University of Mississippi
in 1962, decided to make another personal test of integration in his
home state. To black civil rights workers, Mississippi represented the
worst bigotry in the South. In Mississippi, they feared for their lives.
In fact, King once told his friend Abernathy, "I thought I would be
assassinated in Mississippi, but I got out of Mississippi alive."

Meredith and four friends set off on foot from Memphis, Tennessee, on June 6. Their march was to be a private statement, an individual challenge of their own courage. There would be no press, no
mass demonstration. On the second day, as they approached Her-
nando, Mississippi, Meredith was shot. According to the first news
reports, he had been killed by a shotgun blast from the trees behind
him. In fact, he was only superficially wounded by the sixty pellets
of birdshot. Remaining conscious, he was able to tell the police that
he did not want to be taken to a Mississippi hospital. They took him
back to Memphis.

King and other civil rights leaders hastened to his hospital bed.
"We went to the hospital to see Meredith, and they wouldn't let
anybody in but 'Doc' [Dr. King] and Ralph [Abernathy]," remembers Hosea Williams. The leaders agreed the march should continue. " 'Doc' came out from talking to Meredith and said that he
had agreed in Meredith's room that he would take up the march
and organize other leaders to carry the march on until Meredith was
able to take over control again," says Williams.

"We had an understanding in the movement," explains Andrew
Young, "that if you let people stop you from doing something through
death, then it only encouraged them to kill you whenever they wanted
you to stop doing something. So we were morally obligated, we
felt, to continue that march."

They proposed to begin at the spot where Meredith had been
shot. Meredith agreed, saying, "Yes. This thing is bigger than any
individual. It's bigger than me."

"The shooting of James Meredith in the state of Mississippi is
indicative of the fact that we still have a long, long way to go," King
proclaimed the following day. "Now it's true that we've left Egypt,
but before we arrive safely in the promised land, there are still pro-
digious hilltops of opposition and gigantic mountains of injustice and
resistance before us."

"The James Meredith March against Fear" lasted three weeks
and covered two hundred miles. For Martin King, it was a person-

King attempted to rally the marchers after they were teargassed in Canton, Mississippi.

ally painful journey that included some of his most agonizing and fearful experiences. As they trudged in the scorching summer heat, King overheard some of the young blacks from CORE and SNCC. "I'm not for that nonviolence stuff anymore," one said. "If one of these damned Mississippi crackers touches me, I'm gonna knock the hell out of him." When they sang the familiar anthem of the civil rights movement, "We Shall Overcome," some of the marchers refused to sing the lyric "black and white together" and later told King the song should be changed to "We Shall Overrun."

"The words fell on my ears like strange music from a foreign land," King later wrote. "My hearing was not attuned to the sound of such bitterness." For the first time, those among his own ranks appeared to be questioning the effectiveness of his nonviolent approach.

On the first night of the march, the leaders engaged in a heated debate. "Martin was there. Floyd McKissick was there. Stokely was there. Whitney Young and Roy Wilkins were there," Williams recollects. "Martin was trying to act as a cohesive force to bring everybody together. The Mississippi Freedom Democratic Party had written a manifesto." The manifesto, which insisted among other demands on the use of the word black instead of Negro, alienated some of the older, more conservative leaders. Stokely Carmichael, who had just been elected chairman of SNCC, was urging an all-black march, saying, "We don't need any more white phonies and liberals invading our movement." Williams recalls, "Stokely and those raised so much hell in that meeting and were so nasty and uncooperative that Roy Wilkins said to Martin, 'I'm leaving. I cannot involve myself or the NAACP in a mess like this because we do have white support, white members and we believe in integration.' He gave Martin a number and said, 'I'll be there tomorrow morning by nine o'clock. If there's any change, you can call me.' "

Whitney Young also withdrew. But even the most militant of the leaders were afraid of losing King's support. Succumbing finally to his eloquence, and to his threat to abandon their cause, they agreed that the march would be nonviolent and that white participants would be welcomed.

As the protestors trekked through Mississippi, they attempted to register black voters in each community. Mississippi voter registration lagged markedly behind the rest of the South. In Grenada, they stopped long enough to lead thirteen hundred prospective voters to the courthouse. "When we marched into Grenada, Mississippi, with the Meredith March, that was the most peculiar moment that I can remember in the movement," says Williams, "because no change had taken place in Grenada, Mississippi, in a hundred years. It was just like the Civil War left it. Somebody told me, 'Reverend Williams, do you know they don't hardly let black folks come into the courthouse. They can't drink out of the water fountain. They can't use the rest rooms.' And I made an announcement that we were going over to drink out of the water fountain and use the rest rooms. Now I saw change take place that night. More change took place that night in Grenada, Mississippi, than had taken place in one hundred years."

That night, Carmichael began publicly shouting a new slogan— "Black Power." King felt terribly dismayed and discouraged. He felt "Black Power" was a slogan without hope, a slogan without a program, and he strenuously objected to the violent and provocative context in which it was being shouted. He suggested "Black Equality" instead, but that was rejected by the younger, more radical leaders. He saw the movement becoming permanently and dangerously fragmented. Within a few days, CORE voted to adopt the slogan "Black Power" and the NAACP denounced it. Blacks were forced to choose sides, and moderate whites who had supported the peaceful movement were left out in the cold.

King, distressed by the split, maintained his lifelong belief in nonviolence. "I've decided that I'm going to do battle for my philosophy," he said. "You ought to believe something in life, believe that thing so fervently that you will stand up with it till the end of your days. I can't make myself believe that God wants me to hate. I'm tired of violence . . . and I'm not going to let my oppressor dictate to me what method I must use. . . . We have a power . . . a power that cannot be found in bullets and guns."

When the march reached Greenwood, Carmichael insisted on using the "Black Power" slogan. "We're asking Negroes not to go to Vietnam and fight," he declared, "but to stay in Greenwood and fight here."

SNCC organizer Willie Ricks yelled to the crowd, "What do you want?"

"Black Power!" they responded vehemently.

"What do we want?" he repeated.

"Black Power!" they cried louder with each successive chorus.

Even King's own trusted field marshal, Hosea Williams, took the microphone at the rally and shouted, "Black Power! Get that vote and pin that badge on a black chest! Whip the policeman across the head!'' At this, King jumped in and countered, ''He means with a vote.''

''They know what he means,'' said Carmichael with a sardonic smile.

''There is black power,'' King said. ''I'm all for black power, but as a slogan it is counterproductive.'' The press had already seized on the motto, identifying it with the concept of black supremacy, which to King was as evil as white supremacy. A bitter rivalry broke out between those who shouted ''Black Power'' and those who cried ''Freedom Now,'' long the slogan of the SCLC. The two sides reached an impasse.

Out of respect for King, Carmichael and McKissick finally agreed to drop both rallying cries for the remainder of the march. But Carmichael told King, ''Martin, I deliberately decided to raise the issue on the march in order to give it a national forum and force you to take a stand for Black Power.''

''That's all right,'' King replied, ''I've been used before. One more time won't hurt.''

Except for this internal friction, the march was predominantly peaceful until the group decided to make a detour to Philadelphia, Mississippi, where civil rights workers Goodman, Schwerner, and Chaney had been murdered exactly two years before. Sheriff Rainey and Deputy Price, who were still in command although under indictment for the killings, stood by and watched as white mobs shouted taunts and hurled cherry bombs during King's speech. The police did nothing to stop the fighting that ensued. That night as the battered marchers tried to sleep at their campsite, they were attacked by rifle fire. King announced that he would lead a second larger march on Philadelphia later in the week, and he wired the president appealing for federal marshals to protect the demonstrators when they returned. The White House did not respond.

When the delegation reached Canton on June 24, they attempted to make camp on the grounds of an all-black elementary school. A wall of state and local police closed in, ordering the two thousand marchers to pitch their tents somewhere else. King and the other leaders refused to leave. As they addressed the protestors from a flatbed truck, local and state police moved toward them hurling grenades of tear gas and battering marchers with whips, sticks, and gun butts.

''Dr. King was up on this truck,'' says Williams. ''I got up there

During the Meredith March, Stokely Carmichael first called for "Black Power!" King consistently disavowed the slogan.

*Despite hostile crowds, marchers detoured to
Philadelphia, Mississippi, to pay tribute
to three slain colleagues. Civil rights workers
Andrew Goodman, Michael Schwerner, and James Chaney
had been murdered there exactly two years before.*

Left: *Philadelphia, Mississippi, Courthouse*

Above: *Sheriff Lawrence Rainey.*

"That day in Philadelphia when I was speaking and Rainey was behind me," King recalled, "I just knew I'd never see the end of the day."

on the truck with them. Then the troopers began to close in."

Even those marchers who had scorned nonviolence throughout the journey refrained from striking back. But King and McKissick had to calm a shaken Carmichael. "Don't make your stand here," a hysterical Carmichael sobbed to blacks who were falling all around him. "I just can't stand to see any more people get shot."

"When I got to Canton," recalls Abernathy, who had been in nearby Philadelphia "preaching up a crowd" for the marchers' return there the next day, "we went to the school grounds, and nobody was there. We saw the tear gas cans and everything. And we could still smell the tear gas." When he finally found King at the home of friends where he was staying the night, Abernathy asked what had happened.

"The state troopers had us surrounded, and they started firing tear gas at us." Then King teased, "And Stokely jumped over the rails of the truck like he was a member of the Olympic team."

The next day, King led three hundred nonviolent volunteers back to Philadelphia. It was, according to Abernathy, "one of the most fearful experiences we had in the movement period."

When King and the marchers arrived in Philadelphia to pay tribute to the three slain civil rights workers and to show the white citizens they would not be intimidated by the violence of the previous week, Abernathy thought he had "preached too well." "The white people came and engulfed the thousands of black people," he remembers. "And we were caught in a bind. Dr. King was speaking on the steps of the courthouse. They had locked all the doors to the courthouse, and we could not get in. So, finally, Dr. King said, 'It may be that the murderers of these three young men are here today.' And Deputy Sheriff Price, who later served a sentence, said, 'You're damned right, we're right behind you.' And Dr. King became so afraid. It's the only time I have ever seen him afraid."

"That day in Philadelphia when I was speaking and Rainey was behind me," King later recalled, "I just knew I'd never see [the end of] the day." King stopped his speech abruptly, saying, "Dr. Ralph Abernathy will now lead us in prayer."

Later, as King and Abernathy talked over the events of the day, King admitted to his closest friend, "I was afraid, man. And I apologize because I didn't give you notice, but I had to do something. But Ralph," he continued, "why did you pray with your eyes open?"

"Hell," his friend answered, "do you think you are more brilliant than I am? I had to see what was happening!"

"The Southern white man," explains Abernathy, "can be the biggest racist, but he has respect for God. They are afraid of God. So everybody closed their eyes. This whole mob closed their eyes and began to show respect for God. Because I was looking and I could see it! And when we finished the prayer, which was short, very short—I didn't have to talk to Him much—we didn't start singing because anything could affect them. We marched from those steps, about a thousand people, and not a mumbling word was spoken until we got a block away from the courthouse. That is an example of sticking together and working together in our most fearful hour, and I believe Dr. King would agree."

Meredith resumed his place at the head of the march outside Jackson, the state capital. For the first time, the Kings' two older children, Yoki and Marty, joined their parents for the final leg of the procession from Tougaloo College to the statehouse. By this time, the crowd numbered fifteen thousand—the largest gathering of blacks in the history of Mississippi. On another occasion, King might have been ecstatic. But he was weary and dispirited when he addressed the almost entirely black crowd. The leaders of CORE, SNCC, and the Mississippi Freedom Democrats had refused to let Charles Evers, director of the Mississippi NAACP and brother of the slain Medgar, speak at the rally because of the rift with NAACP. King saw the movement forever torn asunder, saw liberal whites alienated from it, and feared the direction it was taking. Still, he tried to end the March against Fear on a hopeful note, saying, "One day, right here in this state of Mississippi, justice will become a reality for all."

By the summer of 1966, King's concerns were broadening beyond the South. By this time, the forces of political activism in America were becoming polarized around the war in Vietnam. Civil rights and black voter registration were slipping into a subordinate position. Although his primary concern remained with civil rights, King himself had taken a strong anti-Vietnam position. "I am not going to sit by and see the war escalate without saying something about it," he had told his SCLC colleagues. "It is worthless to talk about integrating if there is no world to integrate in. The war in Vietnam must be stopped." His antiwar position brought criticism from the Johnson administration, as well as from other civil rights leaders. But, until the end of his life, King would insist that racial injustice, poverty, and the war were all "inextricably bound together."

With the passage of the Voting Rights Act, poverty became the focal issue for King. As the war in Vietnam escalated, the president's

James Meredith resumed the lead of the march outside Jackson, Mississippi.

Overleaf: *State Capitol, Jackson, Mississippi.*

war on poverty lagged. On both fronts, blacks were sustaining disproportionate casualties. "When we turn to the negative experiences of life," King wrote in *Where Do We Go from Here: Chaos or Community,* "the Negro has a double share. There are twice as many unemployed. The rate of infant mortality . . . among Negroes is double that of whites. The equation pursues Negroes even into war. There were twice as many Negroes as whites in combat in Vietnam at the beginning of 1967, and twice as many Negro soldiers died in action."

King had also begun to turn his attention to the rioting in northern cities and the conditions that were causing it. In Watts the previous summer, he had seen the urgency of the situation in urban ghettos. He also recognized that blacks raised outside the southern tradition were far more hostile and combative. Earlier in the year, King and the SCLC had joined forces with Al Raby's Coordinated Council of Community Organizations (CCCO) to form a Chicago Freedom Movement. The pilot project was aimed at calling attention to ghetto conditions before they exploded. The major objectives were school desegregation and improvement, jobs, and housing.

"The reason Dr. King chose Chicago," says Reverend Jesse Jackson, who had joined the SCLC staff, "is at that time there was a group in Chicago called the Coordinated Council of Community Organizations, about fifty organizations that had come together in order to fight for a better school system and to fight for change here. Dr. King's first inclination was to go to Harlem, but there was so much more organization here, so much more cohesion here, he was lured in this direction."

King had moved his family to a ghetto tenement in Chicago's Lawndale section and commuted between "slumdale," as his colleagues called it, and Atlanta. His neighbors were impressed at his ability to achieve "instant slum clearance" by his mere presence. As soon as his landlord learned who his new tenant was, a crew of workmen hastened to clean up the dwelling and remove long-standing building code violations. Other slumlords in the vicinity followed suit. The *Chicago Sun-Times* editorialized that if King moved from block to block, he might rid the entire city of the blight of slums.

But King empathized with the feeling of powerlessness that pervaded the ghetto and made the creation of a cohesive movement difficult. "Here," says Jackson, "the enemy was not only the Redneck, sometimes it was the black face. It was all those forces that represented the self-interest in perpetuating the evil machine."

One such force was Chicago's consummate politician, Mayor Richard Daley. Instead of denouncing King's campaign, Daley ostensibly supported it. Whatever King proposed, Daley said it was already underway, giving the impression that great strides were being made in the ghetto without King or his movement. The slight gains that resulted, King feared, were dangerous and deceptive. They would dissipate efforts for change without providing long-term solutions.

Designating July 10 as "Freedom Sunday," King kicked off the intensive Chicago crusade, which had so far been fragmented. Speaking to forty-five thousand people at Soldier's Field in ninety-eight-degree heat, he urged blacks to go to jail, if necessary, to eliminate slums. The crowd then marched from Soldier's Field to City Hall to present a program for change to the mayor. Finding Daley absent, King posted his demands on the door—a gesture inspired by his namesake nearly five centuries before. The program called for complete integration of public schools, doubling of the public school budget, construction of low-rent public housing throughout the city, expansion of rapid transit facilities, and support of black banks.

Several days later, rioting broke out on Chicago's West Side. To cool off in the hundred-degree temperature, black children were playing in a fire hydrant. When police came to turn it off, a crowd gathered and a fight broke out between a policeman and one of the youths. With that, gangs of teenagers began stoning police cars, looting white businesses, and hurling Molotov cocktails. Violence continued for three days. Two blacks were killed and hundreds of people were injured, including six policemen. One of the dead was a fourteen-year-old pregnant girl.

King worked with clergymen and community leaders in an attempt to restore peace. "There are thousands of Negro boys and girls packed in this area," he told ministers. "And they turned on the fire hydrant the other night because it was hot. They don't have air-conditioned houses. So often it's seven or eight people living in two rooms. They don't have the comforts and conveniences of life. So they were trying to get a little water. They didn't have a swimming pool, so they had to turn on the fire hydrant, and they were forced

King spoke to the largest gathering
of blacks in the history of Mississippi.

to turn it off. Certainly a little water wouldn't have hurt anything in that situation. . . . I think it's our job to work as passionately to get rid of these conditions as it is to get rid of the violence."

On July 15, Governor Otto Kerner ordered four thousand National Guardsmen to Chicago. King and the other black clergymen had risked their lives in the ghetto trying to calm the youthful rioters. Now they met with Mayor Daley to request federal funds for the construction of swimming pools and recreational facilities for blacks, endeavoring to deal with the cause of the rioting.

The black leaders decided to concentrate their efforts on discrimination in housing. Week after week, they marched on Chicago's all-white neighborhoods. They were greeted by angry mobs hurling bricks and screaming obscenities. On one occasion, the marchers were met by antagonistic whites led by American Nazi Party chief George Lincoln Rockwell. Hit on the head by a brick, King quipped, "Oh, I've been hit so many times I'm immune to it." But he went on to say more seriously, "I've been in many demonstrations all across the South, but I can say that I have never seen, even in Mississippi and Alabama, mobs as hostile and as hate-filled as I've seen in Chicago."

The backlash from the Chicago crusade increased. Even some conservative blacks were condemning King for creating racial tensions and insisting that he stop the marches. "You want us to stop marching, make justice a reality," he retorted. "I don't mind saying to Chicago—or to anybody—I'm tired of marching. I'm tired of marching for something that should have been mine at birth. If you want a moratorium on demonstrations, put a moratorium on injustice. . . . I don't march because I like it. I march because I must, and because I'm a man, and because I'm a child of God."

On August 17, black leaders met for ten hours with city officials, but no agreement was forthcoming. The marches continued. Several days later, black organizers informed Cook County sheriff Richard B. Ogilvie that they planned to march on Cicero. This all-white neighborhood had become a symbol of northern discrimination. In 1951, it was the scene of a bloody riot when a black family tried to move in. Earlier in the summer of 1966, two blacks had gone job hunting there. One was beaten to death. Ogilvie begged King to call off the march. When King refused, the prospect of a major incident provided civic leaders with the incentive to reach an agreement on black demands. Two days before the prospective march, civil rights leaders attended a hastily called meeting with Mayor Daley, Archbishop John Cody, and representatives of the Chicago Real Estate Board, the Chicago Housing Authority, and the business and industrial communities.

Although basically satisfactory to King, the resulting housing agreement was a partial compromise, and militant blacks labeled it a sell-out. They decided to go through with the Cicero march. King felt that if the agreement were honored, it would provide a strong equal housing program. Unfortunately, it never was.

On September 4, SNCC and CORE staged a somewhat anticlimactic march on Cicero. Two hundred blacks, protected by ten times as many National Guardsmen, were attacked so fiercely by flying bottles and rocks that they were forced to retreat to Lawndale.

King meanwhile announced that jobs were now the number one priority in Chicago, and initiated Operation Breadbasket under Reverend Jackson's leadership. This program, which the SCLC had tried with considerable success in Atlanta, would be responsible for finding jobs for the disadvantaged. By boycotting businesses in black neighborhoods that did not hire blacks, the program created more than nine-hundred jobs by the end of the year.

With Operation Breadbasket underway, King closed down his Chicago campaign and returned to Atlanta. With the exception of Reverend Jackson's project, Chicago seemed a failure to most observers. There was growing apathy among local blacks; the NAACP had withdrawn its support; the nation was focused on Vietnam; and there seemed no way to force the white establishment to make good its promises.

Jackson disagrees. "The great effect of the northern movement was to wake up northern black America that they had a problem," he explains. "It wasn't just a matter of coming down South. They needed to come back home and do homework. Dr. King said it would take from three to five years for a sustained nonviolent movement to begin to change the thing. The newspapers in their impatience wanted to make it a three- to five-month movement. It was a three- to five-year movement, and as a result of raising certain basic truths in the Chicago movement, Gary, Indiana, Newark, New Jersey, Cleveland, Ohio, began to reassess their political power and political consciousness. The rock hit the water in Chicago, but the concentric circles shot right across northern America. So I think that the movement was successful."

Nevertheless, the experience left King depressed and deeply troubled. The cry of "Black Power" was louder than ever. The

King and Abernathy were stoned in Cicero, Illinois.

The difficulties of the northern campaign, as well as the escalation of the war in Vietnam, left King deeply troubled.

movement was fractured, never to be put back together. The war in Vietnam escalated daily and was draining manpower, money, and energy that were desperately needed in the domestic war against poverty. He knew he must speak out more fiercely against the war in Vietnam that was costing lives abroad and dissipating the thrust for civil liberties at home. "I can't be silent," he told his aides and friends. "Never again will I be silent."

"We make a great deal about his '*I Have a Dream*' speech," says John Lewis. "But I think his great speech in terms of ideas and philosophy—who we are as a society, as a nation, and as a world community—was the speech he gave at the Riverside Church on Vietnam on April 4, 1967. I think that was his greatest speech really."

In that eloquent and impassioned plea for peace, the Nobel laureate insisted, "Somehow this madness must cease. We must stop now. I speak as a child of God and a brother to the suffering poor of Vietnam. . . . I speak for the poor of America who are paying the double price of smashed hopes at home and death and corruption in Vietnam. I speak as a citizen of the world, for the world as it stands aghast at the path we have taken. I speak as an American to the leaders of my own nation. The great initiative in this war is ours. The initiative to stop it must be ours."

Sanitation workers strike, Memphis, Tennessee.

Chapter Thirteen

Free
at
Last

*Let us not despair. Let us not lose faith
in man and certainly not in God. We must
believe that a prejudiced mind can be changed,
and that man, by the grace of God, can be
lifted from the valley of hate to the high
mountain of love.*

MLK, Jr.

IT BEGAN ON A RAINY miserable day in early 1968. He had known it would come to this. He had always understood what he must do. He had long ago made peace with his God.

The strike in Memphis did not initially attract King's attention. He was busy organizing his Poor People's Campaign. On April 22, he planned to walk with three thousand of the nation's needy to state their case in Washington, D.C. The marchers were to represent all races and creeds. King would shepherd his flock to the nation's capital demanding notice.

But on January 31, when the sanitation workers in Memphis, Tennessee, reported to work, they were sent home because of rain. In their paychecks that week, black employees received wages for only two hours for that day. White workers were paid for the entire day. The black union struck, sending a list of demands to newly elected mayor Henry Loeb. The demands were ignored. When King's longtime friend Reverend James Lawson and the leaders of the strike in Memphis called for an all-out work stoppage on March 28, he agreed to lead the march. If he didn't stop to help the lowliest in Memphis, it made no sense to go to Washington.

Arriving in Memphis on the morning of the demonstration, King was disturbed by the presence of a group of black-power militants. Known as the Invaders, they were interspersed among the peaceful marchers whose dignified banners proclaimed "I AM A MAN." Lawson and his aides assured King the Invaders would not be part of the march. However, the procession had not advanced even three blocks when they heard what sounded like shattering glass.

"What was that?" King asked.

"We heard the breaking of glass," Abernathy remembers vividly. "They were dropping out of the line and committing violence. When Dr. King discovered what had happened, he said to Reverend Lawson, 'Jim, call off this march right now. Call it off *right now!*' And Jim Lawson took the bull horn and called it off and said, 'Disperse. Please go to your homes. Please get out!' "

King's followers, committed to nonviolence, dispersed peacefully. But the militants continued breaking into stores and looting. King's aides, fearing for his life, convinced him to return to his motel. Reverend Bernard Lee managed to stop a car, saying to the young black woman who was driving, "Please, may we use your car to get Dr. King out of this area." She slid over, allowing Lee to drive. King and Abernathy got in the back seat. Abernathy remembers stopping a policeman, asking, "Sir, will you get Dr. King out of here?" When the policeman asked where they wanted to go, King replied, "To the Lorraine Hotel."

"You can't get across there," the officer answered.

"Well, take us to the Peabody," Abernathy suggested. "Take us to the Peabody Hotel."

During the conversation the officer was in communication with police headquarters. "We can't get to the Peabody," he advised. Finally, they heard him say over his radio, "Oh, a nigger was killed?"

"We were astounded to hear this," relates Abernathy. The officer asked, "Was it one of the Invaders?" The confirmation came back, and the officer said, "I'd better take you to the Holiday Inn."

In the disorder that followed the march, a sixteen-year-old black had been shot and killed by police; 60 others were clubbed and wounded; 280 were arrested. Looting and arson continued until the governor of Tennessee ordered four thousand National Guardsmen into the city.

King was shaken and forlorn. In part, he blamed himself for the violence. He and his associates had not planned the march and were unaware of the large militant element in Memphis. Nevertheless, he felt responsible. He felt he had failed.

King was still distressed when he returned to Atlanta to meet with the SCLC staff on Saturday, March 30. At the meeting Abernathy recalls, "We were to decide whether to go back to Memphis, or whether to go to Washington for the Poor People's Campaign. I was presiding over the meeting with Andy Young. And they were debating what we should do. James Bevel and Jesse Jackson had been raising the same questions for a year during the organization for the Poor People's Campaign."

Bevel and Jackson were concerned that the goals of the Poor People's Campaign were amorphous and that without a clear-cut victory in Washington the SCLC would lose credibility. "What is our leverage?" they kept asking. "What is our stick? How do we get out of Washington if we do not win the battle?"

"They had been raising [these questions] in every meeting for a year," explains Abernathy. "Martin got disgusted and got up and came over to me and said, 'Ralph, give me my keys. I am getting out of here.' So I went, too." Sensing King's mood, Abernathy went back to the staff meeting, where he told the others, "When the president of an organization gets troubled, I think the staff ought to come together and quit our bickering and quit our differences."

Hosea Williams took the floor. "I agree with you, Mr. Vice Presi-

*King met with SCLC staff members
Hosea Williams and Andrew Young to
discuss the situation in Memphis.*

dent, one hundred percent." The staff agreed to go to Washington for the Poor People's March—by way of Memphis. King's closely knit lieutenants felt united once again. "Hosea started singing," remembers Abernathy. "And everybody started singing freedom songs. Finally, I called Dr. King and told him to come—that we were together."

Determined to prove that nonviolence was still a viable method of forcing social change, King's organization scheduled a second march in Memphis for April 8. "Andy and Bevel were supposed to leave for Memphis that Sunday afternoon," Abernathy recollects. "Jesse and Hosea were to leave that night to conduct workshops with the people in nonviolence. And prove to Memphis that we could have a nonviolent march because our reputation, SCLC's reputation, had been scarred. Never had we led a violent march before."

Memphis city officials secured a court injunction barring the demonstration. King hoped to get the injunction set aside, but he announced his intention to lead the march regardless. To friends he confided, "Nonviolence is on trial in Memphis."

Asked what effect violence in the upcoming march would have on King, Andrew Young surmised, "I would say that Dr. King would consider it a repudiation of his philosophy and his whole way of life. I don't know when I've seen him as discouraged and depressed."

The weather in Memphis matched King's mood on the night of April 3. Heavy rains were accompanied by tornado warnings. Abernathy had to beg him to address a rally at Mason Temple. He was subdued when he told a crowd of two-thousand cheering supporters about his flight to Memphis that morning. "The pilot said over the public address system, 'We are sorry for the delay, but we have Dr. Martin Luther King on the plane. And to be sure that all of the bags were checked, and to be sure that nothing would be wrong with the plane, we had to check out everything carefully. And we've had the plane protected and guarded all night.' "

He told his audience that when he arrived in Memphis he had begun to hear talk of threats on his life. But threats were not new to King. "A man who won't die for something is not fit to live," he had said on numerous occasions. He had lived for a long time in the shadow of death. He had spoken often of his own death to his intimates. The ever-present danger that had accompanied him since the early days in Montgomery was met with a profound faith. Now, sadly—reflectively—some would later say, prophetically—he took the audience into his confidence. "Like anybody, I would like to live a long life. Longevity has its place. But I'm not concerned about that now. I just want to do God's will. And He's allowed me to go up to the mountain. And I've looked over, and I've seen the promised land. I may not get there with you, but I want you to know tonight that we as a people will get to the promised land. So I'm happy tonight. I'm not worried about anything. I'm not fearing any man. Mine eyes have seen the glory of the coming of the Lord."

He spent almost all of the next day, Thursday, April 4, conferring with his aides in a second-floor room at the Lorraine Hotel on Mulberry Street in Memphis. According to Hosea Williams, "Dr. King really preached us a sermon. He said the only hope of redeeming the soul of this nation was through the power of nonviolence. He talked about the life of Jesus and Gandhi, and he told us, 'I have conquered the fear of death.' "

While he and Abernathy were preparing to go to dinner that same evening, he brought up the subject again. "He told me, 'Ralph, don't ever employ anybody on the staff of SCLC that uses violence to reach our goals, even on a temporary basis.' And I wondered, why is he telling me this? But I concluded that he was telling me only because I was the treasurer of the organization. He didn't want anybody that believed in violence." Those were Martin's last words to his trusted friend and constant companion of almost fifteen years.

While Abernathy finished getting ready to go, King went to the balcony outside his room and talked with several associates in the parking lot below. King chatted amiably with Jesse Jackson, their differences over the Poor People's Campaign forgotten. He asked Jesse to join them for dinner. Jackson introduced "Doc" to a musician, Ben Branch, who was the leader of Jackson's Breadbasket Band. King said, "Yeah, that's my man," and asked Branch to perform a special song for him at that evening's rally. The song was "Take My Hand, Precious Lord." "Play it real pretty," King insisted.

Suddenly, they heard a loud thud—like a firecracker. A single shot from a sniper's high-powered rifle exploded in King's face, ripping off his necktie and smashing him backward onto the concrete balcony. "Oh . . ." It was more an expulsion of breath than an exclamation or an unfinished prayer. Nothing more. Blood spilled from the gaping hole at his neck. Martin Luther King, Jr.—the apostle of nonviolence—was dead. The man whose entire life was a testament to nonviolence—the winner of the Nobel Peace Prize—had died by the assassin's bullet.

At the sound of the shot, the parking lot was suddenly swarming with policemen. James Bevel sank to his knees and prayed. Jesse rushed up the stairs. Andrew Young felt for King's pulse. Somebody tried to stop the bleeding with a towel. Abernathy cradled the head of the man he loved. He, too, had known it would come to this. He, too, had imagined the inevitable. But he had never envisioned being left alone. "I thought that somebody would put a bomb in the car," says Abernathy. "We were always riding together. And it would go off and we would just be killed together. And when it happened, we were together. And the only thing that saved me was Aramis cologne. I would have been in the line of fire, I guess. Because he had finished shaving, and he said, 'Ralph, are you ready to go?' I said 'Yes, but let me put my Aramis on.' He had refreshed himself, and I wanted to refresh myself and smell good, too. And before I could get the Aramis, get it on my hand and get it on my face, I heard what sounded like a firecracker. And I looked, jumped, I looked. And saw him lying on the cold floor of that terrace. And I made my way to him and picked up his head and patted his cheek, the side that the bullet did not enter. And assured him that 'it will be alright, Martin. It will be alright. Don't worry.' And Andy Young was the first person to get up there by me. And Andy said, 'Oh, God!' He said, 'Ralph, it is over!' I became furious. I said, 'Don't you say that. Don't you say that, Andy. It will not be over. It will never be over!' "

With the body of their slain leader at their feet, members of King's entourage pointed to the source of the shot from the balcony of the Lorraine Hotel in Memphis.

Chapter Fourteen

Take My Hand, Precious Lord

*If you want to say that I was a drum major,
say that I was a drum major for justice;
say that I was a drum major for peace; I was
a drum major for righteousness.*

MLK, Jr.

"I'm sorry," the physician said, "We've lost him. It's all over." It was 7:05 p.m. Memphis time. An hour had elapsed since the fatal gunshot.

Abernathy had ridden in the ambulance to St. Joseph's Hospital, where, with Bernard Lee, he stood vigil while doctors futilely fought to save King's life.

Jesse Jackson had been the first to get through to Coretta in Atlanta. Dr. King had been shot, he told her gently. He was alive. "Take the first plane here." And then he added, "He was shot in the shoulder." Atlanta's mayor Ivan Allen rushed to the King home to drive her to the airport. By the time he arrived, Andy Young had called from the hospital. Martin was in critical condition. He had been shot in the neck. But he was not dead. He repeated it. He was not dead. Little by little, they were preparing her. But Martin had done that long ago. When she got to the airport, she learned that her husband was dead. In shock, she decided to go home to her four children. She would leave the next day to claim her husband's body.

"We heard the news that he was dead," remembers the Kings' oldest daughter, Yolanda, who was then twelve. "I think for ten or fifteen minutes I didn't really believe it. . . . Then it kind of dawned on me that Daddy always said to us it can happen, so you've got to be prepared. . . . I was hurt, of course, but I think the reason why I didn't cry was because I kept on thinking about the fact that Daddy wouldn't want me to cry."

"We had waited, agonizing through the nights and days without sleep, startled by nearly any sound, unable to eat, simply staring at our meals," wrote Daddy King. "Suddenly, in a few seconds of radio time, it was over. My first son, whose birth had brought me so much joy that I jumped up in a hall outside the room where he was born and touched the ceiling—the child, the scholar, the preacher, the boy singing and smiling, the son—all of it was gone. And Ebenezer was so quiet; all through the church, as the staff learned what had happened, the tears flowed, but almost completely in silence."

In Washington, President Johnson was in conference with U.S. ambassador to Moscow Llewellyn Thompson when his press aide handed him the first wire bulletin about the shooting. "Get the attorney general to look into this immediately," he said. Minutes later, his secretary, Juanita Roberts, handed him a typed message, "Mr. President, Martin Luther King is dead."

It had already been an extraordinary week for the president. Four days earlier, he had told the war-weary nation that he was halting bombing over parts of Vietnam. And in an effort to end the divisiveness that was tearing our own country apart, he had surprised the world with the announcement that he would not seek reelection in November. Americans had barely had a chance to breathe a sigh of relief, when the news from Memphis rocked the country.

Before the night came to an end, President Johnson, visibly shaken, had made a condolence call to King's widow. In a brief television statement, he said, "America is shocked and saddened by the brutal slaying." He urged unity and peace. He had also dispatched Attorney General Ramsey Clark to Memphis to oversee what was to become the most intensive, most expensive manhunt in the nation's history.

In Memphis, police already had the description of a suspect: a white man with a sharp nose driving a late-model white Mustang. Within minutes of the shooting, they had found a bundle of evidence, including a 30.06 calibre rifle with a telescopic sight and a small suitcase that had been tossed in a doorway near where the shot had reportedly been fired. There were a number of readable fingerprints. Eventually, the suspect would be identified as James Earl Ray, an escaped convict. Two months later he was captured at London's Heathrow Airport. At his trial, he stunned the world by pleading guilty to first degree murder and was sentenced to ninety-nine years in prison. In the absence of a full-blown trial, many questions remained unanswered, as they do to this day. Why did he kill Martin Luther King? Did he act alone, or was he part of a larger conspiracy? Are there others who should have been brought to justice?

With the news of King's death, rioting broke out across the nation. It was both tragic and ironic that his assassination unleashed the furies brooding in the ghettos and touched off the most widespread racial violence in the country's history. King's slaying stunned the nation as no event had since the assassination of John F. Kennedy. For many blacks his murder was a judgment upon his nonviolent philosophy. There could have been no crueler memorial than the violence done in his name.

"When white America killed Dr. King last night she declared war on us," exclaimed Stokely Carmichael. "It would have been better if she had killed Rap Brown . . . or Stokely Carmichael. But when she killed Dr. King, she lost it. . . . He was the one man in our race who was trying to teach our people to have love, compassion, and mercy for white people."

"Dr. Martin Luther King was the last prince of nonviolence," reiterated Floyd McKissick. "Nonviolence is a dead philosophy, and it was not the black people that killed it. It was the white people that killed nonviolence."

The ghetto was on the verge of self-immolation. "It's no longer a question of violence or nonviolence in this day and age," King had said in the last speech of his life. "It is nonviolence or nonexistence." Without his voice, the country seemed to be choosing nonexistence. Before it was over, thirty-nine people died and countless numbers were injured in civil disorders that struck more than 130 American cities. The indiscriminate looting and burning resulted in $45 million worth of damage. There were more than twenty-thousand arrests. In Washington, D.C., Chicago, and Baltimore, more than twenty-thousand regular army troops and nearly fifteen-thousand

National Guardsmen had to be deployed. An additional thirty-thousand guardsmen were called into action in thirteen other states. Curfews were imposed in thirty cities.

Washington, D.C., had not witnessed such a torching since the War of 1812. Helmeted combat troops guarded the White House and a machine gun post defended the Capitol. Within minutes of the news of King's death, blacks in Washington's ghetto found a spokesman and leader. "Go home and get your guns," Stokely Carmichael shouted to them. "When the white man comes he is coming to kill you. I don't want any black blood in the street. Go home and get your gun." Carmichael fed the flames with further violent talk the following day, saying "We have to retaliate for the deaths of our leaders." Asked if he feared for his own life, Stokely told a reporter, "The hell with my life. You should fear for yours. I know I'm going to die."

In a meeting with civil rights leaders the day after the assassination, the president appealed for nonviolence. "No one could doubt what Martin Luther King would want," he told them. "That his death should be the cause for more violence would deny everything he worked for." He said that King's death could lead either to catastrophe or to the final passage of long overdue civil rights legislation and to the rooting out of every trace of racism from white men's hearts.

Hosea Williams immediately called for nonviolence. "Let's not burn America down," he pleaded. "We must—we must—maintain and advocate and promote the philosophy of nonviolence." Considered one of the most militant of King's close associates, Williams continued, "We—those of us with him during his last moments on this earth—are concerned that this country might go into a turmoil that would cause great bloodshed."

From Cincinnati came a reminder from Reverend Fred Shuttlesworth that one of King's philosophies was "Not one hair on the head of one white man shall be harmed by us."

In Chicago, eleven people died. Huge sections of the West Side ghettos were torched by gangs. "When they bury King, we gonna bury Chicago," said one young black. "I thought I was dead until they killed the King," said another. "They killed the King and I came to life. We gonna die fighting. We all gonna die fighting."

One black woman in Chicago was heard begging the looters to stop. "Come out of that store and leave that stuff. You all nothing but bums. Ain't we got enough trouble with our neighborhood

Left. *A flatbed farm cart pulled King's coffin from Ebenezer Baptist Church to Morehead College. For thousands, it was a last chance to march with Martin.*

Above: *Actor Harry Belafonte accompanied Coretta Scott King and her father, Obadiah Scott, to the burial site.*

burning down? Where are those people gonna live after you burn them down?'' But hers, and all the voices of reason, were lost in the vengeful grief of the ghetto.

In Minneapolis, a black man vowed to kill the first white person he saw and shot his white neighbor to death. "My King is dead," he sobbed, after pumping a half dozen bullets into his victim.

From the midst of the violence came the tributes from black and white alike. "White America began to understand what Martin Luther King was all about at the moment of his death," says Young.

"No words of mine can fill the void of the eloquent voice that has been stilled," President Johnson said the day after King's death. "But this I do believe deeply: The dream of Dr. Martin Luther King has not died with him. Men who are white, men who are black, must and will now join together as never in the past to let all the forces of divisiveness know that America shall not be ruled by the bullet, but only by the ballot of free and just men."

The president announced that Sunday, April 7, would be a day of national mourning. Flags flew at half-mast. Services were held in King's honor at churches throughout America. In Washington Cathedral, Reverend Walter Fauntroy preached to a congregation of four thousand, including President Johnson, Vice President Hubert Humphrey, the entire Supreme Court, members of the cabinet, prominent members of the legislature, and nearly every eminent black in the civil rights movement. "Forgive us for our individual and our corporate sins that have led us inevitably to this tragedy," he prayed. "Forgive us. God, please forgive us."

At his own Ebenezer Baptist Church, where King would have preached the Palm Sunday sermon, his brother A. D. King stood in his place. With tears in his eyes, and his father, Martin Luther King, Sr., by his side, he called America a "dying nation" and urged the country to "come to your hour now." The most emotional moment came when the choir soloist sang "Take My Hand, Precious Lord," the spiritual that had been on King's mind when he died.

In the days following his assassination, tributes were paid by heads of state and world leaders, and expressions of sympathy came from all over the world. Pope Paul VI said that the "cowardly and atrocious" killing "weighed on the conscience of mankind."

"I weep for Mrs. King and for her children for this senseless, senseless act of hate which took away a man who preached love and hope," said Jacqueline Kennedy. "When will our country learn that to live by the sword is to perish by the sword?"

In a measure that appeared to be an impossible dream before the assassination, the United States House of Representatives rushed out an historic fair-housing act and sent it to President Johnson for his signature. Illinois Republican John B. Anderson, whose pivotal vote got the bill out of the House Rules Committee, said to the thunderous applause of his colleagues, "I legislate today not out of fear but out of deep concern for the America I love."

The NAACP's Roy Wilkins said, "Dr. King was a symbol of the nonviolent civil rights protest movement. He was a man of peace, of dedication, of great courage. His senseless assassination solves nothing. It will not stay the civil rights movement; it will instead spur it to greater activity."

On April 8, the day King had planned to restage his march in Memphis, the widowed Coretta and her three oldest children stoically led a silent memorial march through that city in his honor. More than fifteen thousand people from all over the United States took part. Ralph Abernathy, who at King's request had succeeded him as head of the SCLC, marched with Mrs. King.

Mrs. King addressed the crowd outside the Memphis City Hall. As she would prove many times in the future, she was prepared to take up her late husband's cause: "We must carry on because this is the way he would have wanted it to have been. . . . We are going to continue his work to make all people truly free and to make every person feel that he is a human being." Coretta's strength was admired by a sorrowing world. But it came as no surprise to her friends or to her husband's associates. They knew she had always lent a quiet support and calming spirit to everything Martin had undertaken.

King's body lay in state in a chapel on the campus of Spelman College in Atlanta and subsequently at his family's own Ebenezer Church. Mourners of all races, religions, and social classes—the lowliest and the mightiest—came to pay their respects, often waiting hours to file past his casket. "We really lost somebody, didn't we?" grieved one old lady. "I'm hoping Easter Sunday he'll rise again!"

Vast crowds, estimated as high as one hundred thousand, surrounded Ebenezer Baptist Church on April 9 during the memorial service. A hundred and twenty million television viewers watched at home. Ebenezer's pews could seat only eight hundred people. So many celebrities attended that some of King's own staff members were shut outside. The congregation included six presidential aspirants, twenty-three senators, forty-seven congressmen, three governors, a Supreme Court justice. Robert Kennedy, Jacqueline

Above: *Reverend Jesse Jackson served as one of King's pallbearers.*

Right: *King's widow and brother, Reverend A. D. King, at the memorial service at Morehouse College.*

Kennedy, Harry Belafonte, Sammy Davis, Jr., and Jackie Robinson were among those in attendance.

Ralph Abernathy officiated. As he led the family down the aisle, he intoned, "I am the resurrection and the life; he that believeth in me, though he were dead, yet shall he live. . . .

"We gather here this morning in one of the darkest hours in the history of the black people of this nation," he said, "in one of the darkest hours in the history of all mankind."

Many wept when the tape of the last sermon King had delivered at the Ebenezer Baptist Church was played during the service. They heard King's voice—stilled but not silenced—say, "If any of you are around when I have to meet my day, I don't want a long speech. I'd like somebody to mention that day that Martin Luther King, Jr., tried to give his life for others. I'd like somebody to say that day that Martin Luther King, Jr., tried to love somebody. I want you to say that day that I tried to be like and to walk with them. I won't have any money to leave behind. I won't have the fine luxurious things of life to leave behind. But I just want to leave a committed life behind. Then my living will not be in vain."

"Martin Luther King spoke with the tongues of men and of angels," his former teacher Dr. L. Harold De Wolfe told the mourners. "Now those eloquent lips are stilled. . . . It is now for us, all the millions of the living who care, to take up his torch of love. It is for us to finish his work, to end the awful destruction in Vietnam, to root out every trace of prejudice from our lives, to bring the massive powers of this nation to aid the oppressed and to heal the hate-scarred world."

The march that followed King's funeral epitomized the many he had made in life. It was a cortege of a sort America had never seen before—not for a black man or for any man. A cross of white flowers led the way. Two mules pulled his African mahogany coffin on a flatbed farm cart three and a half miles from the church to Morehouse College. Thousands followed behind. It was their last chance to march with Martin. They were silent at first. But as they flowed into the shuttered streets of downtown Atlanta, the old songs welled up. In measured cadence, "We Shall Overcome" mingled with the muffled clippity-clop of the mule-drawn cart.

On the Morehouse campus, his teacher and friend Dr. Benjamin Mays spoke a eulogy. "He drew no distinction between the high and the low," said Mays, "none between the rich and the poor. He believed especially that he was sent to champion the cause of the man farthest down. He would probably have said, 'If death had to

*Robert and Ethel Kennedy were
among the many who offered their
personal condolences to Mrs. King.
Two months later, Kennedy was
assassinated in Los Angeles.*

come, I am sure there was no greater cause to die for than fighting
to get a just wage for the garbage collectors.' "

All that was left was the ride to the all-black South View Cemetery, where he was buried beside his grandparents. At the interment
rites, Reverend Abernathy prayed, "The cemetery is too small for
his spirit, but we submit his body to the ground. The grave is too
narrow for his soul, but we commit his body to the ground. No
coffin, no crypt, no stone can hold his greatness. But we submit his
body to the ground."

The epitaph on the hastily carved marble tombstone was derived
from the old Negro spiritual, "Free at last; free at last; thank God
Almighty, I'm free at last."

Chapter Fifteen

King
Remembered

*Over the bleached bones and
jumbled residues of numerous civilizations
are written the pathetic words: "Too
late." . . . We still have a choice today:
nonviolent coexistence or violent coannihilation.
This may well be mankind's last chance to
choose between chaos and community.*

MLK, Jr.

History had spoken through Martin Luther King, Jr., and chosen him to lead his people out of bondage. When leadership was thrust upon him, King flowered in the pulpit of protest. A product of the southern Baptist church, his contribution was uniquely southern and Christian. His philosophy of nonviolent protest was a blend of Christian vision and tactical necessity stitched together in the streets of Montgomery, Birmingham, and Selma. Throughout the South, King and the talented young ministers of the SCLC had transformed numberless insignificant black churches into outposts of revolution. They were conscious provocateurs, bent on stretching the country's racial nerves to the breaking point. King's rolling, hypnotic baritone converted soul-weary southern blacks into nonviolent warriors. His colleagues jested appreciatively that his vast following was so devoted that he could discuss Platonic dogma among illiterates and evoke heartfelt cries of "Amen."

Rarely has one individual, espousing so difficult a philosophy, served as the catalyst for so much significant social change. King did not wait for evolution to occur naturally. He incited evolution. There are few men of whom it can be said their lives changed the world. But at his death, the American South hardly resembled the land where King was born. In the twelve years between the Montgomery bus boycott and King's assassination, Jim Crow was legally eradicated in the South. Blacks took their places alongside fellow Americans on buses, at the lunch counter, in the work place, and in the legislatures.

With the passage of the Civil Rights Act of 1964 and the Voting Rights Act of 1965, blacks began immediately to enter the political arena. In 1963, there were fewer than 50 black elected officials in the entire South. By 1984, that number had grown to 3,498, more than all the rest of the nation combined. With their new voting strength, black mayoral candidates won in 48 American cities in 1970. By 1984, black mayors were governing 255 cities. Today, the city of Atlanta is governed by blacks. Nearly every Black Belt county in Alabama has a black sheriff. Mississippi has more black elected officials than any other state. Twenty years after King's Selma campaign, two of that city's five city council members are black, as is one of the district's two state senators. Selma has a black assistant police chief, as well as a black school board member.

On the federal level, political progress has come more slowly. In 1970, there were nine black representatives and one black senator in the U.S. Congress. In 1984, the number of black representatives had more than doubled to twenty-one, but there was not a single black senator. Nevertheless, Reverend Jesse Jackson's candidacy for president of the United States in 1984 proved to blacks and whites alike how far we have come because Martin Luther King passed a Voting Rights Act in the streets of Selma. Jackson's candidacy was more than simply the first time a black had run for the nation's highest office. He gathered 19 percent of the vote in the primaries of Georgia and Alabama and won outright in Louisiana with 42 percent. He, and by extension all black Americans, became serious and significant political contenders.

Ironically, this kind of progress has led veteran black leaders to fear that they have been *too* successful. They worry that an entire generation of blacks has grown up today who cannot imagine that the state of the nation was ever otherwise. They are troubled that no black in his twenties has emerged as a post-desegregation leader. And, most of all, they worry that the blacks' remarkable legal and social gains have not been translated into economic and political leverage. "We were so successful," explains Reverend C. T. Vivian, "that it's impossible for young blacks to understand what has happened. We've never learned to institutionalize our horror."

"Everything has changed and nothing has changed," says Reverend Joseph Lowery, president of the SCLC.

In the sixties, discrimination meant police dogs and bombings of black homes and churches. Today, civil rights leaders note a more subtle form of discrimination. Voting districts are gerrymandered to dilute minority strength, the Justice Department is lackadaisical in enforcing the law, retrogressive court decisions undermine affirmative action programs. Habit keeps segregation alive in the rural South, even while black professionals pour out of Atlanta's office buildings, work alongside whites in a Birmingham restaurant, and control dozens of courthouses across the South. Where the laws are not carried out to the utmost, old customs linger like pernicious memories. In small towns throughout the South even today, blacks are directed to separate rest rooms in public buildings or sit in separate waiting rooms in the offices of white doctors and dentists. Still, too, in Selma, as in hundreds of cities in the North and South alike, the country club admits no black members. Neighborhoods in many cities remain largely segregated, and there is little social interaction between the races.

King had prophesied that, although the promised land was within sight, the journey would still be long and arduous. "The real cost

JOE T. SMITHERMAN
MAYOR

Left: *Joseph M. McGrue, assistant police chief of Selma, Alabama, with Mayor Joe T. Smitherman in 1985. Smitherman was mayor twenty years earlier, during the Selma marches.*

Above: *Reverend C. T. Vivian, director of affiliates for the SCLC, heads the National Anti-Klan Network and the Black Action Strategies and Information Center (BASIC). "We often say we have been too successful," explains Vivian. "It was so successful that it's impossible for young blacks to understand what has happened."*

lies ahead," he wrote in his last book, published posthumously. "The stiffening of white resistance is a recognition of that fact. The discount education given Negroes will in the future have to be purchased at full price if quality education is to be realized. Jobs are harder and costlier to create than voting rolls. The eradication of slums housing millions is complex far beyond integrating buses and lunch counters." He knew at the time of his death that the next great battle the black man would have to wage was the battle for economic justice. He believed that to end poverty, America must make a radical commitment to redistribution of wealth. And he knew that this concept was a stiletto as threatening to America as the one that nearly pierced his heart in a Harlem department store.

His analysis has proven true. His disciples—and all Americans of conscience—know that poverty remains as a cancer in American life. "In the days ahead," he wrote, "we must not consider it unpatriotic to raise certain basic questions about our national character. We must begin to ask, 'Why are there forty million poor people in a nation overflowing with such unbelievable affluence?' Why has our nation placed itself in the position of being God's military agent on earth? . . . Why have we substituted the arrogant undertaking of policing the whole world for the high task of putting our own house in order?

"All these questions remind us that there is a need for a radical restructuring of the architecture of American society. For its very survival's sake, America must reexamine old presuppositions and release itself from many things that for centuries have been held sacred. For the evils of racism, poverty and militarism to die, a new set of values must be born."

At the root of King's civil rights conviction was an even more profound faith in the basic goodness of man and the great potential of American democracy. He evoked the best in Americans. He enabled us to visualize our country as it is supposed to be—the America of our grade school history books. "I have a dream this evening," he told the people of Detroit, "that one day we will recognize the words of Jefferson that all men are created equal and they are endowed by their creator with some inalienable rights and among these are life, liberty and the pursuit of happiness."

With this vision, he gave us a philosophy of Christian love, based on the Judeo-Christian tradition that is interwoven in the fabric of American idealism. "Love thy neighbor," he urged. He spoke of the redemptive force of suffering, of brotherhood, of the power of

Georgia senator Julian Bond and Georgia state representative
George Brown were among the first blacks elected to the
Georgia General Assembly. "If Dr. King were alive today,
I think he would be addressing international questions
and economic questions as much as race questions,"
says Senator Bond.

*Atlanta mayor Andrew Young:
"His important legacy is that
human problems no matter how big
can be solved. They can be
solved without destroying either
person or property. And organizing
to solve those problems is an
on-going process."*

nonviolence. He was a Christian preacher who lived what he preached. But he was also a man of action. Within his Christian philosophy, he forged a technique for social action—nonviolent resistance—and he tested it in the crucible of racist America. Using this tool, he incited a peaceful revolution.

He was, more than any individual, the voice of America's black revolution. At times he dominated the stage so completely, people thought he *was* the civil rights movement. In fact, he was not. But the movement never could have gone so far without him. He gave expression to the black man's anguish; eloquence to his humiliation; dignity to his struggle for equality. And he gave the weakest and the most humble a weapon powerful enough to withstand, and even overcome, the cruel forces of segregation. The weapon was nonviolence.

Martin King's dream is still a dream deferred in many ways. But he was no idle dreamer. He left us not only a goal, but also a means of achieving that goal. To each of us as individuals he passed the burden of defending human rights in our country and around the world. And he gave us a blueprint to follow in exercising our responsibility. In his last book, *Where Do We Go from Here: Chaos or Community,* King established his priorities for social programs and social progress. Education, human rights, economic justice, and peace were among his chief concerns. They remain our most urgent priorities today.

For his humanity; for his leadership; for his love of his fellow man regardless of the color of his skin or his position in life; and for his wisdom in showing all of us how we must live and think and act if we are to achieve the promise of the American dream, King *is* remembered.

"He was a moment in the conscience of man," eulogized Harry Belafonte.

To many millions of black Americans, King was the prophet of their crusade for racial equality. "I can't see what's different between him and the Messiah. That's just the truth about it, and I am not a real religious man," says Rufus Lewis, a member of Montgomery's Dexter Avenue Baptist church.

"A man of his magnitude will not soon pass this way again," said Gary, Indiana's first black mayor, Richard Hatcher.

To eighty-nine-year-old Virge Parker of Atlanta, Georgia, the change King wrought upon the face of the South was nothing less than a miracle. "When I was young, the Ku Klux Klan hung a boy 'cause a white girl say he looked at her," recalled Parker. "Driving down to Florida one time, a man refused to sell me gas. Just 'cause I was black. But Dr. King, he changed a lot of things. He said there'll come a time when white chillun and black chillun will play together. That happened. And all the folks down at city hall, they all black folks. I'm sure glad I lived long enough to see things turn out the way they did. All those bad old days, they gone with the wind."

"God only puts on the face of the earth a leader like that once in a number of years. He's never had more than one Moses at a time," says Reverend T. J. Jimerson, a lifelong friend and associate.

"He made popular the idea," says Georgia senator Julian Bond, "that individuals are capable of changing their situation. Through the protests of the 1960s, it was demonstrated that black people could do this, and now you see larger groups of people doing it. Women, farmers and others have seized upon nonviolent protest as a means of advancing their cause. Although Martin Luther King didn't invent sit-in demonstrations and didn't invent mass marches, he made them available to the larger body of the American population."

Andrew Young, mayor of Atlanta, echoes Bond's sentiments. "I think his important legacy is that human problems, no matter how big, can be solved."

"In him the word became flesh and dwelt among men," says Reverend Jesse Jackson, one of King's closest associates and one of those disciples upon whom the mantle of leadership has fallen. "He didn't just talk brotherhood; he was a brother. He didn't just talk friendship; he was a friend. He didn't just talk change; he was a change agent. He didn't wish for change; he changed things. I see him in all of those lights. Thinking about him is like thinking about the prism, the sun shining through a glass from as many angles as you look. You know there is another set of rays, and as many angles as you think about Dr. King, there is yet another set of angles with which to analyze him."

"I don't think America has yet learned to appreciate the greatness of Martin Luther King, Jr.," says Reverend Shuttlesworth. "I think that his life will be constantly revealing itself to us."

Appendix

Letter from Birmingham Jail

April 16, 1963
Birmingham, Alabama

My Dear Fellow Clergymen:

While confined here in the Birmingham city jail, I came across your recent statement calling my present activities "unwise and untimely." Seldom do I pause to answer criticism of my work and ideas. If I sought to answer all the criticisms that cross my desk, my secretaries would have little time for anything other than such correspondence in the course of the day, and I would have no time for constructive work. But since I feel that you are men of genuine good will and that your criticisms are sincerely set forth, I want to try to answer your statement in what I hope will be patient and reasonable terms.

I think I should indicate why I am here in Birmingham, since you have been influenced by the view which argues against "outsiders coming in." I have the honor of serving as president of the Southern Christian Leadership Conference, an organization operating in every southern state, with headquarters in Atlanta, Georgia. We have some eighty-five affiliated organizations across the South, and one of them is the Alabama Christian Movement for Human Rights. Frequently we share staff, educational, and financial resources with our affiliates. Several months ago the affiliate here in Birmingham asked us to be on call to engage in a nonviolent direct-action program if such were deemed necessary. We readily consented, and when the hour came we lived up to our promise. So I, along with several members of my staff, am here because I was invited here. I am here because I have organizational ties here.

But more basically, I am in Birmingham because injustice is here. Just as the prophets of the eighth century B.C. left their villages and carried their "thus saith the Lord" far beyond the boundaries of their home towns, and just as the Apostle Paul left his village of Tarsus and carried the gospel of Jesus Christ to the far corners of the Greco-Roman world, so am I compelled to carry the gospel of freedom beyond my own home town. Like Paul, I must constantly respond to the Macedonian call for aid.

Moreover, I am cognizant of the interrelatedness of all communities and states. I cannot sit idly by in Atlanta and not be concerned about what happens in Birmingham. Injustice anywhere is a threat to justice everywhere. We are caught in an inescapable network of mutuality, tied in a single garment of destiny. Whatever affects one directly, affects all indirectly. Never again can we afford to live with the narrow, provincial "outside agitator" idea. Anyone who lives inside the United States can never be considered an outsider anywhere within its bounds.

You deplore the demonstrations taking place in Birmingham. But your statement, I am sorry to say, fails to express a similar concern for the conditions that brought about the demonstrations. I am sure that none of you would want to rest content with the superficial kind of social analysis that deals merely with effects and does not grapple with underlying causes. It is unfortunate that demonstrations are taking place in Birmingham, but it is even more unfortunate that the city's white power structure left the Negro community with no alternative.

In any nonviolent campaign there are four basic steps: collection of the facts to determine whether injustices exist; negotiation; self-purification; and direct action. We have gone through all these steps in Birmingham. There can be no gainsaying the fact that racial injustice engulfs this community. Birmingham is probably the most thoroughly segregated city in the United States. Its ugly record of brutality is widely known. Negroes have experienced grossly unjust treatment in the courts. There have been more unsolved bombings of Negro homes and churches in Birmingham than in any other city in the nation. These are the hard, brutal facts of the case. On the basis of these conditions, Negro leaders sought to negotiate with the city fathers. But the latter consistently refused to engage in good-faith negotiation.

Then, last September, came the opportunity to talk with leaders of Birmingham's economic community. In the course of the negotiations, certain promises were made by the merchants—for example, to remove the stores' humiliating racial signs. On the basis of these promises, the Reverend Fred Shuttlesworth and the leaders of the Alabama Christian Movement for Human Rights agreed to a moratorium on all demonstrations. As the weeks and months went by, we realized that we were the victims of a broken promise. A few signs, briefly removed, returned; the others remained.

As in so many past experiences, our hopes had been blasted, and the shadow of deep disappointment settled upon us. We had no alternative except to prepare for direct action, whereby we would present our very bodies as a means of laying our case before the conscience of the local and the national community. Mindful of the difficulties involved, we decided to undertake a process of self-purification. We began a series of workshops on nonviolence, and we repeatedly asked ourselves, "Are you able to accept blows without retaliation?" "Are you able to endure the ordeal of jail?" We decided to schedule our direct-action program for the Easter season, realizing that except for Christmas, this is the main shopping period of the year. Knowing that a strong economic-withdrawal program would be the by-product of direct action, we felt that this would be the best time to bring pressure to bear on the merchants for the needed change.

Then it occurred to us that Birmingham's mayoral election was coming up in March, and we speedily decided to postpone action until after election day. When we discovered that the Commissioner of Public Safety, Eugene "Bull" Connor, had piled up enough votes to be in the run-off, we decided again to postpone action until the day after the run-off so that the demonstrations could not be used to cloud the issues. Like many others, we waited to see Mr. Connor defeated, and to this end we endured postponement after postponement. Having aided in this community need, we felt that our direct-action program could be delayed no longer.

You may well ask, "Why direct action? Why sit-ins, marches, and so forth? Isn't negotiation a better path?" You are quite right in calling for negotiations. Indeed, this is the very purpose of direct action. Nonviolent direct actions seeks to create such a crisis and foster such a tension that a community which has constantly refused to negotiate is forced to confront the issue. It seeks so to dramatize the issue that it can no longer be ignored. My citing the creation of tension as part of the work of the nonviolent-resister may sound rather shocking. But I must confess that I am not afraid of the word "tension." I have earnestly opposed violent tension, but there is a type of constructive, nonviolent tension which is necessary for growth. Just as Socrates felt that it was necessary to create a tension in the mind so that individuals could rise from the bondage of myths and half-truths to the unfettered realm of creative analysis and objective appraisal, so must we see the need for nonviolent gadflies to create the kind of tension in society that will help men rise from the dark depths of prejudice and racism to the majestic heights of understanding and brotherhood.

The purpose of our direct-action program is to create a situation so crisis-packed that it will inevitably open the door to negotiation. I therefore concur with you in your call for negotiation. Too long has our beloved Southland been bogged down in a tragic effort to live in monologue rather than dialogue.

One of the basic points in your statement is that the action that I and my associates have taken in Birmingham is untimely. Some have asked: "Why didn't you give the new city administration time to act?" The only answer that I can give to this query is that the new Birmingham administration must be prodded about as much as the outgoing one, before it will act. We are sadly mistaken if we feel that the election of Albert Boutwell as mayor will bring the millennium to Birmingham. While Mr. Boutwell is a much more gentle person than Mr. Connor, they are both segregationists, dedicated to maintenance of the status quo. I have hoped that Mr. Boutwell will be reasonable enough to see the futility of massive resistance to desegregation. But he will not see this without pressure from devotees of civil rights. My friends, I must say to you that we have not made a single gain in civil rights without determined legal and nonviolent pressure. Lamentably, it is an historical fact that privileged groups seldom give up their privileges voluntarily. Individuals may see the moral light and voluntarily give up their unjust posture; but, as Reinhold Niebuhr has reminded us, groups tend to be more immoral than individuals.

We know through painful experience that freedom is never voluntarily given by the oppressor; it must be demanded by the oppressed. Frankly, I have yet to engage in a direct-action campaign that was "well-timed" in view of those who have not suffered unduly from the disease of segregation. For years now I have heard the word "Wait!" It rings in the ear of every Negro with piercing familiarity. This "Wait" has almost always meant "Never." We must come to see, with one of our distinguished jurists, that "justice too long delayed is justice denied."

We have waited for more than 340 years for our constitutional and God-given rights. The nations of Asia and Africa are moving with jetlike speed toward gaining political independence, but we still creep at horse-and-buggy pace toward gaining a cup of coffee at a lunch counter. Perhaps it is easy for those who have never felt the stinging darts of segregation to say, "Wait." But when you have seen vicious mobs lynch your mothers and fathers at will and drown your sisters and brothers at whim; when you have seen hate-filled policemen curse, kick, and even kill your black brothers and sisters; when you see the vast majority of your twenty million Negro brothers smothering in an airtight cage of poverty in the midst of an affluent society; when you suddenly find your tongue twisted and your speech stammering as you seek to explain to your six-year-old daughter why she can't go to the public amusement park that has just been advertised on television, and see tears welling up in her eyes when she is told that Funtown is closed to colored children, and see ominous clouds of inferiority beginning to form in her little mental sky, and see her beginning to distort her personality by developing an unconscious bitterness toward white people; when you have to concoct an answer for a five-year-old son who is asking, "Daddy, why do white people treat colored people so mean?"; when you take a cross-country drive and find it necessary to sleep night after night in the uncomfortable corners of your automobile because no motel will accept you; when you are humiliated day in and day out by nagging signs reading "white" and "colored"; when your first name become "nigger," your middle name becomes "boy" (however old you are) and your last name becomes "John," and your wife and mother are never given the respected title "Mrs."; when you are harried by day and haunted by night by the fact that you are a Negro, living constantly at tiptoe stance, never quite knowing what to expect next, and are plagued with inner fears and outer resentments; when you are forever fighting a degenerating sense of "nobodiness"—then you will understand why we find it difficult to wait. There comes a time when the cup of endurance runs over, and men are no longer willing to be plunged into the abyss of despair. I hope, sirs, you can understand our legitimate and unavoidable impatience.

You express a great deal of anxiety over our willingness to break laws. This is certainly a legitimate concern. Since we so diligently urge people to obey the Supreme Court's decision of 1954 outlawing segregation in the public schools, at first glance it may seem rather paradoxical for us consciously to break laws. One may well ask: "How can you advocate breaking some laws and obeying others?" The answer lies in the fact that there are two types of laws: just and unjust. I would be the first to advocate obeying just laws. One has not only a legal but a moral responsibility to obey just laws. Conversely, one has a moral responsibility to disobey unjust laws. I would agree with St. Augustine that "an unjust law is no law at all."

Now, what is the difference between the two? How does one determine whether a law is just or unjust? A just law is a man-made code that squares with the moral law or the law of God. An unjust law is a code that is out of harmony with the moral law. To put it in the terms of St. Thomas Aquinas: An unjust law is a human law that is not rooted in eternal law and natural law. Any law that uplifts human personality is just. Any law that degrades human personality is unjust. All segregation statutes are unjust because segregation distorts the soul and damages the personality. It gives the segregator a false sense of superiority and the segregated a false sense of inferiority. Segregation, to use the terminology of the Jewish philosopher Martin Buber, substitutes an "I-it" relationship for an "I-thou" relationship and ends up relegating persons to the status of things. Hence segregation is not only politically, economically, and sociologically unsound, it is morally wrong and sinful. Paul Tillich has said that sin is separation. Is not segregation an existential expression of man's tragic separation, his awful estrangement, his terrible sinfulness? Thus it is that I can urge men to obey the 1954 decision of the Supreme Court, for it is morally right; and I can urge them to disobey segregation ordinances, for they are morally wrong.

Let us consider a more concrete example of just and unjust laws. An unjust law is a code that a numerical or power majority group compels a minority group to obey but does not make binding on itself. This is *difference* made legal. By the same token, a just law is a code that a majority compels a minority to follow and that it is willing to follow itself. This is *sameness* made legal.

Let me give another explanation. A law is unjust if it is inflicted on a minority that, as a result of being denied the right to vote, had no part in enacting or devising the law. Who can say that the legislature of Alabama which set up that state's segregation laws was democratically elected? Throughout Alabama all sorts of devious methods are used to prevent Negroes from becoming registered voters, and there are some counties in which, even though Negroes constitute a majority of the population, not a single Negro is registered. Can any law enacted under such circumstances be considered democratically structured?

Sometimes a law is just on its face and unjust in its application. For instance, I have been arrested on a charge of parading without a permit. Now there is nothing wrong in having an ordinance which requires a permit for a parade. But such an ordinance becomes unjust when it is used to maintain segregation and to deny citizens the First-Amendment privilege of peaceful assembly and protest.

I hope you are able to see the distinction I am trying to point out. In no sense do I advocate evading or defying the law, as would the rabid segregationist. That would lead to anarchy. One who breaks an unjust law must do so openly, lovingly, and with a willingness to accept the penalty. I submit that an individual who breaks a law that conscience tells him is unjust, and who willingly accepts the penalty of imprisonment in order to arouse the conscience of the community over its injustice, is in reality expressing the highest respect for law.

Of course, there is nothing new about this kind of civil disobedience. It was evidenced sublimely in the refusal of Shadrach, Meshach, and Abednego to obey the laws of Nebuchadnezzar, on the ground that a higher moral law was at stake. It was practiced superbly by the early Christians, who were willing to face hungry lions and the excruciating pain of chopping blocks rather than submit to certain unjust laws of the Roman Empire. To a degree, academic freedom is a reality today because Socrates practiced civil disobedience. In our own nation, the Boston Tea Party represented a massive act of civil disobedience.

We should never forget that everything Adolf Hitler did in Germany was "legal" and everything the Hungarian freedom fighters did in Hungary was "illegal." It was "illegal" to aid and comfort a Jew in Hitler's Germany. Even so, I am sure that, had I lived in Germany at the time, I would have aided and comforted my Jewish brothers. If today I lived in a Communist country where certain principles dear to the Christian faith are suppressed, I would openly advocate disobeying that country's anti-religious laws.

I must make two honest confessions to you, my Christian and Jewish brothers. First, I must confess that over the past few years I have been gravely disappointed with the white moderate. I have almost reached the regrettable conclusion that the Negro's great stumbling block in his stride toward freedom is not the White Citizen's Counciler or the Ku Klux Klanner, but the white moderate, who is more devoted to "order" than to justice; who prefers a negative peace which is the absence of tension to a positive peace which is the presence of justice; who constantly says, "I agree with you in the goal you seek, but I cannot agree with your methods of direct action": who paternalistically believes he can set the timetable for another man's freedom; who lives by a mythical concept of time and who constantly advises the Negro to wait for a "more convenient season." Shallow understanding from people of good will is more frustrating than absolute misunderstanding from people of ill will. Lukewarm acceptance is much more bewildering than outright rejection.

I had hoped that the white moderate would understand that law and order exist for the purpose of establishing justice and that when they fail in this purpose they become the dangerously structured dams that block the flow of social progress. I had hoped that the white moderate would understand that the present tension in the South is a necessary phase of the transition from an obnoxious negative peace, in which the Negro passively accepted his unjust plight, to a substantive and positive peace, in which all men will respect the dignity and worth of human personality. Actually, we who engage in nonviolent direct action are not the creators of tension. We merely bring to the surface the hidden tension that is already alive. We bring it out in the open, where it can be seen and dealt with. Like a boil that can never be cured so long as it is covered up but must be opened with all its ugliness to the natural medicines of air and light, injustice must be exposed, with all the tension its exposure creates, to the light of human conscience and the air of national opinion, before it can be cured.

In your statement you assert that our actions, even though peaceful, must be condemned because they precipitate violence. But is this a logical assertion? Isn't this like condemning a robbed man because his possession of money precipitated the evil act of robbery? Isn't this like condemning Socrates because his unswerving commitment to truth and his philosophical inquiries precipitated the act by the misguided populace in which they made him drink hemlock? Isn't this like condemning Jesus because his unique God-consciousness and never-ceasing devotion to God's will precipitated the evil act of crucifixion? We must come to see that, as the federal courts have consistently affirmed, it is wrong to urge an individual to cease his efforts to gain his basic constitutional rights because the quest may precipitate violence. Society must protect the robbed and punish the robber.

I had also hoped that the white moderate would reject the myth concerning time in relation to the struggle for freedom. I have just received a letter from a white brother in Texas. He writes, "All Christians know that the colored people will receive equal rights eventually, but it is possible that you are in too great a religious hurry. It has taken Christianity almost two thousand years to accomplish what it has. The teachings of Christ take time to come to earth." Such an attitude stems from a tragic misconception of time, from the strangely irrational notion that there is something in the very flow of time that will inevitably cure all ills. Actually, time itself is neutral; it can be used either destructively or constructively. More and more I feel that the people of ill will have used time much more effectively than have the people of good will. We will have to repent in this generation not merely for the hateful words and actions of the bad people, but for the appalling silence of the good people. Human progress never rolls in on wheels of inevitability; it comes through the tireless efforts of men willing to be co-workers with God, and without this hard work, time itself becomes an ally of the forces of stagnation. We must use time creatively, in the knowledge that the time is always ripe to do right. Now is the time to make real the promise of democracy and transform our pending national elegy into a creative psalm of brotherhood. Now is the time to lift our national policy from the quicksand of racial injustice to the solid rock of human dignity.

You speak of our activity in Birmingham as extreme. At first I was rather disappointed that fellow clergymen would see my nonviolent efforts as those of an extremist. I began thinking about the fact that I stand in the middle of two opposing forces in the Negro community. One is a force of complacency, made up in part of Negroes who, as a result of long years of oppression, are so drained of self-respect and a sense of "somebodiness" that they have adjusted to segregation, and in part of a few middle-class Negroes who, because of a degree of academic and economic security and because in some ways they profit by segregation, have become insensitive to the problems of the masses. The other force is one of bitterness and hatred, and it comes perilously close to advocating violence. It is expressed in the various black nationalist groups that are springing up across the nation, the largest and best-known being Elijah Muhammad's Muslim movement. Nourished by the Negro's frustration over the continued existence of racial discrimination, this movement is made up of people who have lost faith in America, who have absolutely repudiated Christianity, and who have concluded that the white man is an incorrigible "devil."

I have tried to stand between these two forces, saying that we need emulate neither the "do-nothingism" of the complacent nor the hatred and despair of the black nationalist. For there is the more excellent way of love and nonviolent protest. I am grateful to God that, through the influence of the Negro church, the way of nonviolence became an integral part of our struggle.

If this philosophy had not emerged, by now many streets of the South would, I am convinced, be flowing with blood. And I am further convinced that if our white brothers dismiss as "rabble-rousers" and "outside agitators" those of us who employ nonviolent direct action, and if they refuse to support our nonviolent efforts, millions of Negroes will, out of frustration and despair, seek solace and security in black-nationalist ideologies—a development that would inevitably lead to a frightening racial nightmare.

Oppressed people cannot remain oppressed forever. The yearning for freedom eventually manifests itself, and that is what has happened to the American Negro. Something within has reminded him of his birthright of freedom, and something without has reminded him that it can be gained. Consciously or unconsciously, he has been caught up by the *Zeitgeist,* and with his black brothers of Africa and his brown and yellow brothers of Asia, South America, and the Caribbean, the United States Negro is moving with a sense of great urgency toward the promised land of racial justice. If one recognizes this vital urge that has engulfed the Negro community, one should readily understand why public demonstrations are taking place. The Negro has many pent-up resentments and latent frustrations, and he must release them. So let him march; let him make prayer pilgrimages to the city hall; let him go on freedom rides—and try to understand why he must do so. If his repressed emotions are not released in nonviolent ways, they will seek expression through violence; this is not a threat but a fact of history. So I have not said to my people, "Get rid of your discontent." Rather, I have tried to say that this normal and healthy discontent can be channeled into the creative outlet of nonviolent direct action. And now this approach is being termed extremist.

But though I was initially disappointed at being categorized as an extremist, as I continued to think about the matter I gradually gained a measure of satisfaction from the label. Was not Jesus an extremist for love: "Love your enemies, bless them that curse you, do good to them that hate you, and pray for them which despitefully use you, and persecute you." Was not Amos an extremist for justice: "Let justice roll down like waters and righteousness like an ever-flowing stream." Was not Paul an extremist for the Christian gospel: "I bear in my body the marks of the Lord Jesus." Was not Martin Luther an extremist: "Here I stand; I cannot do otherwise, so help me God." And John Bunyan: "I will stay in jail to the end of my days before I make a butchery of my conscience." And Abraham Lincoln: "This nation cannot survive half slave and half free." And Thomas Jefferson: "We hold these truths to be self-evident, that all men are created equal. . . ." So the question is not whether we will be extremists, but what kind of extremists we will be. Will we be extremists for hate or for love? Will we be extremists for the preservation of injustice or for the extension of justice? In that dramatic scene on Calvary's hill three men were crucified. We must never forget that all three were crucified for the same crime—the crime of extremism. Two were extremists for immorality, and thus fell below their environment. The other, Jesus Christ, was an extremist for love, truth, and goodness, and thereby rose above his environment. Perhaps the South, the nation, and the world are in dire need of creative extremists.

I had hoped that the white moderate would see this need. Perhaps I was too optimistic; perhaps I expected too much. I suppose I should have realized that few members of the oppressor race can understand the deep groans and passionate yearnings of the oppressed race, and still fewer have the vision to see that injustice must be rooted out by strong, persistent, and determined action. I am thankful, however, that some of our white brothers in the South have grasped the meaning of this social revolution and committed themselves to it. They are still all too few in quantity, but they are big in quality. Some—such as Ralph McGill, Lillian Smith, Harry Golden, James McBride Dabbs, Ann Braden, and Sarah Patton Boyle— have written about our struggle in eloquent and prophetic terms. Others have marched with us down nameless streets of the South. They have languished in filthy, roach-infested jails, suffering the abuse and brutality of policemen who view them as "dirty nigger-lovers." Unlike so many of their moderate brothers and sisters, they have recognized the urgency of the moment and sensed the need for powerful "action" antidotes to combat the disease of segregation.

Let me take note of my other major disappointment. I have been so greatly disappointed with the white church and its leadership. Of course, there are some notable exceptions. I am not unmindful of the fact that each of you has taken some significant stands on this issue. I commend you, Reverend Stallings, for your Christian stand on this past Sunday, in welcoming Negroes to your worship service on a nonsegregated basis. I commend the Catholic leaders of this state for integrating Spring Hill College several years ago.

But despite these notable exceptions, I must honestly reiterate that I have been disappointed with the church. I do not say this as one of those negative critics who can always find something wrong with the church. I say this as a minister of the gospel, who loves the church; who was nurtured in its bosom; who has been sustained by its spiritual blessings and who will remain true to it as long as the cord of life shall lengthen.

When I was suddenly catapulted into the leadership of the bus protest in Montgomery, Alabama, a few years ago, I felt we would be supported by the white church. I felt that the white ministers, priests, and rabbis of the South would be among our strongest allies. Instead, some have been outright opponents, refusing to understand the freedom movement and misrepresenting its leaders; all too many others have been more cautious than courageous and have remained silent behind the anesthetizing security of stained-glass windows.

In spite of my shattered dreams, I came to Birmingham with the hope that the white religious leadership of this community would see the justice of our cause and, with deep moral concern, would serve as the channel through which our just grievances could reach the power structure. I had hoped that each of you would understand. But again I have been disappointed.

I have heard numerous southern religious leaders admonish their worshipers to comply with a desegregation decision because it is the law, but I have longed to hear white ministers declare: "Follow this decree because integration is morally right and because the Negro is your brother." In the midst of blatant injustices inflicted upon the Negro, I have watched white churchmen stand on the sideline and mouth pious irrelevancies and sanctimonious trivialities. In the midst of a mighty struggle to rid our nation of racial and economic injustice, I have heard many ministers say: "Those are social issues, with which the gospel has no real concern." And I have watched many churches commit themselves to a completely other-worldly religion which makes a strange, un-Biblical distinction between body and soul, between the sacred and the secular.

I have traveled the length and breadth of Alabama, Mississippi, and all the other southern states. On sweltering summer days and crisp autumn mornings I have looked at the South's beautiful churches with their lofty spires pointing heavenward. I have beheld the impressive outlines of her massive religious-education buildings. Over and over I have found myself asking: "What kind of people worship here? Who is their God? Where were their voices when the lips of Governor Barnett dripped with words of interposition and nullification?

Where were they when Governor Wallace gave a clarion call for defiance and hatred? Where were their voices of support when bruised and weary Negro men and women decided to rise from the dark dungeons of complacency to the bright hills of creative protest?"

Yes, these questions are still in my mind. In deep disappointment I have wept over the laxity of the church. But be assured that my tears have been tears of love. Yes, I love the church. How could I do otherwise? I am in the rather unique position of being the son, the grandson, and the great-grandson of preachers. Yes, I see the church as the body of Christ. But, oh! How we have blemished and scarred that body through social neglect and through fear of being nonconformists.

There was a time when the church was very powerful—in the time when the early Christians rejoiced at being deemed worthy to suffer for what they believed. In those days the church was not merely a thermometer that recorded the ideas and principles of popular opinion; it was a thermostat that transformed the mores of society. Whenever the early Christians entered a town, the people in power became disturbed and immediately sought to convict the Christians for being "disturbers of the peace" and "outside agitators." But the Christians pressed on, in the conviction that they were "a colony of heaven," called to obey God rather than man. Small in number, they were big in commitment. They were too God-intoxicated to be "astronomically intimidated." By their effort and example they brought an end to such ancient evils as infanticide and gladiatorial contests.

Things are different now. So often the contemporary church is a weak, ineffectual voice with an uncertain sound. So often it is an archdefender of the status quo. Far from being disturbed by the presence of the church, the power structure of the average community is consoled by the church's silent—and often even vocal—sanction of things as they are.

But the judgment of God is upon the church as never before. If today's church does not recapture the sacrificial spirit of the early church, it will lose its authenticity, forfeit the loyalty of millions, and be dismissed as an irrelevant social club with no meaning for the twentieth century. Every day I meet young people whose disappointment with the church has turned into outright disgust.

Perhaps I have once again been too optimistic. Is organized religion too inextricably bound to the status quo to save our nation and the world? Perhaps I must turn my faith to the inner spiritual church, the church within the church, as the true *ekklesia* and hope of the world. But again I am thankful to God that some noble souls from the ranks of organized religion have broken loose from the paralyzing chains of conformity and joined us as active partners in the struggle for freedom. They have left their secure congregations and walked the streets of Albany, Georgia, with us. They have gone down the highways of the South on tortuous rides for freedom. Yes, they have gone to jail with us. Some have been dismissed from their churches, have lost the support of their bishops and fellow ministers. But they have acted in the faith that right defeated is stronger than evil triumphant. Their witness has been the spiritual salt that has preserved the true meaning of the gospel in these troubled times. They have carved a tunnel of hope through the dark mountain of disappointment.

I hope the church as a whole will meet the challenge of this decisive hour. But even if the church does not come to the aid of justice, I have no despair about the future. I have no fear about the outcome of our struggle in Birmingham, even if our motives are at present misunderstood. We will reach the goal of freedom in Birmingham and all over the nation, because the goal of America is freedom. Abused and scorned though we may be, our destiny is tied up with America's destiny. Before the pilgrims landed at Plymouth, we were here. For more than two centuries, our forebears labored in this country without wages; they made cotton king; they built the homes of their masters while suffering gross injustice and shameful humiliation—and yet out of a bottomless vitality they continued to thrive and develop. If the inexpressible cruelties of slavery could not stop us, the opposition we now face will surely fail. We will win our freedom because the sacred heritage of our nation and the eternal will of God are embodied in our echoing demands.

Before closing I feel impelled to mention one other point in your statement that has troubled me profoundly. You warmly commended the Birmingham police force for keeping "order" and "preventing violence." I doubt that you would have so warmly commended the police force if you had seen its dogs sinking their teeth into unarmed, nonviolent Negroes. I doubt that you would so quickly commend the policemen if you were to observe their ugly and inhumane treatment of Negroes here in the city jail; if you were to watch them push and curse old Negro women and young Negro girls; if you were to see them slap and kick old Negro men and young boys; if you were to observe them, as they did on two occasions, refuse to give us food because we wanted to sing our grace together. I cannot join you in your praise of the Birmingham police department.

It is true that the police have exercised a degree of discipline in handling the demonstrators. In this sense they have conducted themselves rather "nonviolently" in public. But for what purpose? To preserve the evil system of segregation. Over the past few years I have consistently preached that nonviolence demands that the means we use must be as pure as the ends we seek. I have tried to make clear that it is wrong to use immoral means to attain moral ends. But now I must affirm that it is just as wrong, or perhaps even more so, to use moral means to preserve immoral ends. Perhaps Mr. Connor and his policemen have been rather nonviolent in public, as was Chief Pritchett in Albany, Georgia, but they have used the moral means of nonviolence to maintain the immoral end of racial injustice. As T. S. Eliot has said, "The last temptation is the greatest treason: To do the right deed for the wrong reason."

I wish you had commended the Negro sit-inners and demonstrators of Birmingham for their sublime courage, their willingness to suffer, and their amazing discipline in the midst of great provocation. One day the South will recognize its real heroes. They will be the James Merediths, with the noble sense of purpose that enables them to face jeering and hostile mobs, and with the agonizing loneliness that characterizes the life of the pioneer. They will be old, oppressed, battered Negro women, symbolized in a seventy-two-year-old woman in Montgomery, Alabama, who rose up with a sense of dignity and with her people decided not to ride segregated buses, and who responded with ungrammatical profundity to one who inquired about her weariness: "My feets is tired, but my soul is at rest." They will be the young high school and college students, the young ministers of the gospel and a host of their elders, courageously and nonviolently sitting in at lunch counters and willingly going to jail for conscience sake. One day the South will know that when these disinherited children of God sat down at lunch counters, they were in reality standing up for what is best in the American dream and for the most sacred values in our Judaeo-Christian heritage, thereby bringing our nation back to those great wells of democracy which were dug deep by the founding fathers in their formulation of the Constitution and the Declaration of Independence.

Never before have I written so long a letter. I'm afraid it is much too long to take your precious time. I can assure you that it would have been much shorter if I had been writing from a comfortable desk, but what else can one do when he is alone in a narrow jail cell, other than write long letters, think long thoughts, and pray long prayers?

If I have said anything in this letter that overstates the truth and indicates an unreasonable impatience, I beg you to forgive me. If I have said anything that understates the truth and indicates my having a patience that allows me to settle for anything less than brotherhood, I beg God to forgive me.

I hope this letter finds you strong in the faith. I also hope that circumstances will soon make it possible for me to meet each of you, not as an integrationist or a civil rights leader but as a fellow clergyman and a Christian brother. Let us all hope that the dark clouds of racial prejudice will soon pass away and the deep fog of misunderstanding will be lifted from our fear-drenched communities, and in some not too distant tomorrow the radiant stars of love and brotherhood will shine over our great nation with all their scintillating beauty.

YOURS FOR THE CAUSE OF PEACE AND BROTHERHOOD,
MARTIN LUTHER KING, JR.

Chronology

Key Events in the Life of Martin Luther King, Jr., and the Nonviolent Civil Rights Movement

1929

Martin Luther King, Jr., is born to Reverend and Mrs. Martin Luther King, Sr., on January 15 in Atlanta, Georgia.

1947

King is licensed to preach and begins assisting his father, who is pastor of Ebenezer Baptist Church in Atlanta.

1948

King is ordained as a Baptist minister on February 25. In June, he graduates from Morehouse College in Atlanta and receives a scholarship to study divinity at Crozer Theological Seminary in Chester, Pennsylvania.

1949

While studying at Crozer, King attends a lecture by Dr. Mordecai Johnson on the life and work of Mahatma Gandhi and is inspired to delve deeper into the teachings of the Indian social philosopher.

1951

King graduates from Crozer with a Bachelor of Divinity degree. He is class valedictorian and winner of the Pearl Plafker Award for most outstanding student. In September, he begins doctoral studies in theology at Boston University, where he studies personalism with Edgar Sheffield Brightman and L. Harold De Wolf.

1953

King marries Coretta Scott at her family's home in Marion, Alabama, on June 18.

1954

In May, the *Brown v. Board of Education* decision paves the way for school desegregation as the Supreme Court of the United States unanimously rules racial segregation in public schools unconstitutional. The same month, King accepts a position as pastor of the Dexter Avenue Baptist Church in Montgomery, Alabama. On October 31, he is installed as the church's twentieth pastor.

1955

Having completed his dissertation, King is awarded his Ph.D. from Boston University. On November 17, Yolanda Denise (Yoki), the Kings' first child, is born. Less than one month later, on December 5, the Montgomery bus boycott begins after Mrs. Rosa Parks, a seamstress, is arrested for refusing to give up her seat to a white person. King is elected president of the newly formed Montgomery Improvement Association and assumes leadership of the boycott, which will last 381 days.

1956

The Kings' home is bombed on January 30. Although Mrs. King and Yolanda are at home with a friend, no one is injured.

In early February, the University of Alabama in Tuscaloosa is ordered by the Supreme Court to admit its first black student, Autherine Lucy. When white students demonstrate, Lucy is suspended from the University of Alabama for "reasons of safety." A federal district judge orders her reinstated. When she is expelled again, she makes no further effort to enroll, and the university remains segregated until 1963.

On February 21, King is indicted, along with twenty-four other ministers and more than one hundred other blacks, for conspiring to prevent the Montgomery bus company from operation of business.

A United States District Court rules on June 4 that racial segregation on Alabama's city bus lines is unconstitutional. On November 13, the United States Supreme Court unanimously upholds the decision.

On December 21, blacks and whites in Montgomery ride for the first time on previously segregated buses.

1957

More than sixty black ministers, committed to a southern civil rights movement, respond to King's call for a meeting. In Atlanta on January 9 and 10, they form the organization that will become the Southern Christian Leadership Conference (SCLC).

While King and Rev. Ralph Abernathy are in Atlanta for the meeting, Abernathy's home and church are bombed in Montgomery. Three other Baptist churches and the home of a white minister are also bombed in response to the victory of the bus boycott.

On February 14, the SCLC meets formally for the first time in New Orleans. King is unanimously elected president.

On May 17, three years to the day after the *Brown v. Board of Education* decision, King participates with other civil rights leaders in a Prayer Pilgrimage to Washington. He delivers his first major national address, calling for black voting rights. The next month, he meets with Vice-President Richard Nixon.

On September 9, Congress passes the 1957 Civil Rights Act, the first civil rights legislation since Reconstruction. The act created the Civil Rights Commission, established the Civil Rights Division of the Justice Department, and empowered the federal government to seek court injunctions against obstruction of voting rights.

The same month, President Dwight D. Eisenhower federalizes the Arkansas National Guard to escort nine black students to Little Rock Central High, a previously all-white high school. A thousand paratroopers are sent to restore order, and troops remain on campus for an entire school year. When the U.S. Supreme Court refuses to delay desegregation, Little Rock schools are closed for the 1958–59 school year. When they reopen, they are integrated.

Martin Luther III, the Kings' second child and first son, is born in Montgomery on October 23.

1958

On June 23, King, along with Roy Wilkins of the NAACP and A. Philip Randolph of the AFL-CIO, meets with President Eisenhower.

King is arrested on September 3 in front of the Montgomery Recorder's Court and charged with loitering. The charge is later changed to "failure to obey an officer." The following day, he is convicted. He decides to go to jail rather than pay the fine. Over King's objection, the fine is paid by Montgomery Police Commissioner Clyde C. Sellers.

On September 20, King is stabbed in the chest by Mrs. Izola Curry in a Harlem department store while autographing his newly published book, *Stride toward Freedom: The Montgomery Story*.

1959

In early February, Dr. and Mrs. King depart for a monthlong trip to India, where, as the guests of Prime Minister Nehru, they study Gandhi's techniques of nonviolence.

King submits his resignation as pastor of Dexter Avenue Baptist Church on November 29. He will join his father as co-pastor of Ebenezer Baptist Church in Atlanta, where the SCLC has its headquarters.

1960

The sit-in movement begins on February 1 at a Woolworth lunch counter in Greensboro, North Carolina. In an effort to desegregate lunch counters, movies, hotels, libraries, and other segregated facilities, it spreads rapidly throughout the country.

On February 17, a warrant is issued for King's arrest on charges that he did not pay his 1956 and 1958 Alabama state income taxes. In May, an all-white jury in Montgomery, Alabama, acquits King of the tax-evasion charge.

On May 6, the 1960 Civil Rights Act is signed. The new legislation authorizes judges to appoint referees to help blacks register and vote.

King meets with Senator John F. Kennedy, candidate for president of the United States, on June 24 to discuss racial concerns.

In October, King is arrested in a sit-in at a major Atlanta department store. The charges are subsequently dropped, and all of the jailed demonstrators except King are released. King is held on a charge of violating probation in a previous traffic arrest case. He is sentenced to four months of hard labor and transferred to DeKalb County Jail in Decatur, Georgia, and from there to Reidsville State Prison. Only after Senator Kennedy intervenes is he released on two thousand–dollars bail.

In a 7-to-2 decision in December, the U.S. Supreme Court holds that discrimination in bus terminal restaurants operated for the service of interstate passengers is a violation of the Interstate Commerce Act.

1961

On January 10, Charlayne Hunter and Hamilton Holmes become the first black students to enroll at the University of Georgia in Athens. The event is peaceful.

The Kings' third child, Dexter Scott, is born on January 30.

In March, the Congress of Racial Equality (CORE), along with SNCC and SCLC, announces a new campaign—the Freedom Rides. The first Freedom Riders depart from Washington, D.C., on May 4. One bus is burned and stoned in Anniston, Alabama, on May 14. The same day, riders are attacked in Birmingham. When they arrive in Montgomery on May 20, the ensuing violence leads to martial law. In Jackson, Mississippi, the riders are arrested and spend forty to sixty days in Parchman Penitentiary.

In November, in large measure as a result of the Freedom Rides, the Interstate Commerce Commission bans segregation on buses, trains, and supportive facilities.

On December 15, King arrives in Albany, Georgia, to help the local movement in its fight to desegregate public facilities. The following day King is arrested and charged with obstructing the sidewalk and parading without a permit.

1962

King is arrested at a prayer vigil at the Albany City Hall on July 27 and jailed on charges of failure to obey an officer, disorderly conduct, and obstructing the sidewalk. The Albany Movement is generally unsuccessful in its effort to force desegregation of public facilities.

Two are killed and many are injured as James Meredith attempts to enroll at Ole Miss—the University of Mississippi in Oxford—in September. He is enrolled by Supreme Court order and escorted onto the campus by U.S. marshals federalized by President John Kennedy.

On October 16, King meets with President Kennedy at the White House.

1963

Bernice Albertine, the fourth child of Dr. and Mrs. King, is born on March 28.

Mass demonstrations begin in Birmingham, Alabama, on April 3 to protest segregation of public facilities. On April 12, King and other ministers are arrested by Police Commissioner Eugene ("Bull") Connor. King is placed in solitary confinement. While imprisoned, King writes his famous "Letter from Birmingham Jail," explaining the need for nonviolent civil disobedience.

When school children join the protests in Birmingham in early May, Bull Connor orders the use of fire hoses and police dogs to halt the youthful protestors. The nation is shocked by the photographs of police brutality.

On May 10, a biracial agreement is announced in Birmingham to desegregate public accommodations, increase job opportunities for blacks, and provide amnesty to those arrested.

White segregationists react violently to the agreement. On May 11, a bomb explodes at the home of King's brother, Reverend A. D. King, in Birmingham. A second explosion blasts King's headquarters in the Gaston Motel. In response, blacks in Birmingham riot. Two hundred and fifty state troopers are sent to keep peace.

On May 20, the Supreme Court rules Birmingham's segregation ordinances unconstitutional.

When black students Vivian Malone and James Hood attempt to register at the University of Alabama on June 11, Alabama governor George Wallace carries out a 1962 campaign promise to "stand in the schoolhouse door" to prevent integration of Alabama's schools. Wallace confronts Deputy Attorney General Nicholas Katzenbach, who brought a proclamation from President Kennedy. At a second confrontation later the same day, Wallace withdraws and allows the black students to register.

The following day, June 12, in Jackson, Mississippi, NAACP state chairman Medgar Evers is shot to death as he returns home. Byron de la Beckwith of Greenwood, Mississippi, is later charged with the murder, but his two trials both result in mistrials.

The March on Washington, on August 28, becomes the largest and most dramatic civil rights demonstration in history. More than 250,000 marchers, including 60,000 whites, fill the mall from the Lincoln Memorial to the Washington Monument. King and other civil rights leaders meet with President Kennedy in the White House. King's "I Have a Dream" speech is the high point of the event.

On September 15, a bomb explodes during Sunday school in Birmingham's Sixteenth Avenue Baptist Church, killing four little girls, aged eleven to fourteen. This is the twenty-first bombing incident against blacks in Birmingham in eight years. No perpetrators are ever found.

President Kennedy is assassinated in Dallas, Texas, on November

22. Upon assuming office, President Johnson urges the speedy passage of Kennedy's civil rights bill as a fitting tribute to the murdered president.

1964

Time magazine names King "Man of the Year" in its January 3 issue.

In April, demonstrations begin in St. Augustine, Florida. Mrs. Malcolm Peabody, the mother of the governor of Massachusetts, is arrested. In May, King is jailed for demonstrating in St. Augustine, where protests meet violent reaction from white segregationists.

Three young civil rights workers, James Chaney, Michael Schwerner, and Andrew Goodman, are reported missing on June 21, while working on a summer voter registration project in Philadelphia, Mississippi.

King witnesses the signing of the 1964 Civil Rights Act by President Lyndon Johnson on July 2. This is the most far-reaching civil rights legislation since Reconstruction. Among other provisions, it guarantees blacks the right to vote and access to public accommodations. It also authorizes the federal government to sue to desegregate public facilities and schools.

In July, riots erupt in New York City's Harlem after a fifteen-year-old black boy is shot by an off-duty policeman. The initial rioting is followed by uprisings throughout the summer in the Brownsville section of Brooklyn, as well as in Bedford-Stuyvesant; Rochester, N.Y.; New Jersey; Chicago; and Philadelphia.

On August 4, the bodies of civil rights workers James Chaney, Andrew Goodman, and Michael Schwerner are found by FBI agents in a shallow grave near Philadelphia, Mississippi. All three had been shot. Chaney had been brutally beaten. Neshoba county sheriff Lawrence Rainey and his deputy, Cecil Price, are arrested for conspiring to violate the Civil Rights Code. Ultimately, Price and six others are convicted. Sheriff Rainey is found not guilty.

In September, New York City begins busing students to end segregation in public schools.

King is awarded the Nobel Peace Prize in Oslo, Norway, on December 10. He is the twelfth American, third black, and, at age thirty-five, the youngest person to win the coveted prize.

1965

The Selma campaign is initiated on February 2, when King is arrested for demonstrating as part of the SCLC's voter registration drive. Several days later, a federal district court bans the literacy test and other technicalities used against black voter applicants, and on February 9, King meets with President Johnson at the White House to discuss voting rights.

Jimmie Lee Jackson, a twenty-six-year-old black man, is fatally shot by state troopers during a demonstration in Marion, Alabama, on February 18.

Three days later, on February 21, Malcolm X, Black Muslim leader, is assassinated at a rally of his followers in the Audubon Ballroom in New York. Eventually three blacks are convicted of his murder.

On March 7, demonstrators in Selma are beaten by state patrolmen as they attempt to cross the Edmund Pettus Bridge on a march from Selma to the state capitol in Montgomery.

That evening, Reverend James Reeb and two other white Unitarian ministers are beaten by white segregationists in Selma. Reeb dies two days later. The three men who are later indicted for the murder are all acquitted by a Selma jury.

President Johnson addresses a joint session of Congress on March 15 to appeal for the passage of the Voting Rights Bill, which he submits two days later. In the televised address, he uses the slogan of the nonviolent movement—"We Shall Overcome."

On March 21, King and three thousand protestors begin a five-day march from Selma to the Alabama state capitol in Montgomery. By agreement, only three hundred are allowed to cross the Edmund Pettus Bridge and continue the entire way to the state capitol. They are escorted by hundreds of army troops and national guardsmen. In Montgomery, they are met by twenty-five thousand marchers.

Mrs. Viola Liuzzo, a civil rights worker from Detroit, is shot to death while driving returning marchers back to Selma on March 25. The next day, President Johnson denounces the Ku Klux Klan and announces the arrests of four Klan members in connection with the murder. On March 30, the House Un-American Activities Committee opens a full investigation of the Klan and its "shocking crimes."

On August 6, President Johnson signs the 1965 Voting Rights Act.

Six days of rioting break out in Watts, the black ghetto of Los Angeles, on August 11, leaving thirty-five dead. More than thirty-five hundred people are arrested in one of the worst riots in the nation's history.

1966

In January, Julian Bond, newly elected to the Georgia legislature, is denied his seat on the grounds of disloyalty because he opposes the war in Vietnam. Robert Weaver, named head of the Department of Housing and Urban Development, becomes the first black to serve in a presidential cabinet, and Constance Baker Motley becomes the first black woman to be named a federal judge.

In February, King and his family move into a tenement apartment in Chicago to initiate the Chicago Project. The SCLC joins forces with Al Raby's Coordinating Council of Community Organizations. King meets with Black Muslim leader Elijah Muhammad in Chicago.

On May 4, more than 80 percent of Alabama's registered blacks vote in the Alabama Democratic primary. The first major black vote since Reconstruction causes sheriffs James Clark of Selma and Al Lingo of Birmingham to lose their offices.

James Meredith is shot on June 6—the first day of his 220-mile "March Against Fear" from Memphis, Tennessee, to Jackson, Mississippi. King and other civil rights leaders decide to continue the march. In Greenwood, Mississippi, Stokely Carmichael, the newly elected head of SNCC, and Willie Ricks use the slogan "Black Power" for the first time in front of reporters.

Designating July 10 "Freedom Sunday," King initiates a drive to make Chicago an "open city," demanding an end to discrimination in housing, schools, and employment.

Rioting erupts on Chicago's West Side on July 12. Two black youths are killed. King begins negotiations with Mayor Richard Daley. Illinois governor Otto Kerner orders four thousand National Guardsmen to Chicago.

On August 5, King is assaulted with stones as he leads marchers through Chicago's Southwest Side. SNCC and CORE march on Chicago's Cicero suburb on September 4. King and SCLC do not participate. Two hundred blacks, protected by National Guardsmen, are fiercely attacked and forced to retreat.

1967

On February 15, President Johnson proposes the 1967 Civil Rights Act to Congress, including a strong open-housing provision. The bill does not pass, but similar provisions are later incorporated in the 1968 Civil Rights Act.

At a news conference in New York on April 16, King warns that at least ten cities "could explode in racial violence this summer" because conditions that caused riots last summer still exist.

On June 2, riots begin in the Roxbury section of Boston. More than 60 people are injured, and nearly 100 are arrested. Before the summer is over, riots occur in Newark, Detroit, Milwaukee, and more than 30 other American cities. In Detroit alone, 43 die and 324 are injured.

In an historic ruling on June 19, a federal judge orders schools in Washington, D.C., to end *de facto* segregation by the fall semester.

On July 26, King, A. Philip Randolph, Roy Wilkins, and Whitney Young issue a joint statement appealing for an end to the riots, which "have proved ineffective and damaging to the civil rights cause and the entire nation."

The following day, the president appoints Governor Kerner of Illinois and Mayor Lindsay of New York to head a riot commission to investigate the cause of disorders and to recommend means of preventing or containing them in the future.

On November 7, Carl Stokes is elected mayor of Cleveland, Ohio, the first black elected mayor of a major U.S. city.

On November 27, King announces the inception of the Poor People's Campaign, focusing on jobs and freedom for poor people—black and white.

1968

In his State of the Union address on January 17, President Johnson calls for programs to train and hire the hardcore unemployed. Subsequently, he sends a special message to Congress on civil rights.

On February 12, sanitation workers go on strike in Memphis, Tennessee.

King leads a demonstration in Memphis on March 28 in support of the striking sanitation workers. When the march becomes violent, one black is killed and more than fifty people are injured. King leaves Memphis distressed over the violence. He returns April 3 in the hopes of leading a peaceful march. He tells a crowd at the Memphis Masonic Temple, "I may not get there with you, but I want you to know tonight that we as a people will get to the promised land."

The following day, April 4, Martin Luther King, Jr., is assassinated on the balcony of the Lorraine Hotel in Memphis. He dies at St. Joseph's Hospital of a gunshot wound in the neck. James Earl Ray is eventually captured and convicted of the murder and sentenced to ninety-nine years in prison.

Rioting, burning, and looting erupt in cities throughout the United States upon the news of King's assassination. Rioting in Washington's black section is the worst in the capital's history.

The president declares April 7 a national day of mourning for King.

On April 8, Coretta Scott King assumes her husband's place leading a massive silent march through the streets of Memphis.

Thousands of people attend King's funeral on April 9 at Ebenezer Baptist Church in Atlanta. Millions more watch on television.

The 1968 Civil Rights Act prohibiting racial discrimination in the sale or rental of housing is passed by Congress on April 11.

Index